DEDICATION

This book is dedicated to my very good friend, Claudia Scott. She is a true mentor and encourages me to think outside the box. She has no problem telling me when something I write is good and, conversely, when she is sure she is going to like the set and costumes. Thank you, Claudia, for everything. Especially making me sit back many times… Many MANY times, in such surprise and wonder that I say to myself, "I can do better. I have to learn faster."

Table of Contents

SPIRITUAL HYPOCHONDRIA............................1
LIKE A SOFT WIND..13
KIDNAPPED...28
IT'S NOT YOU..43
OUT OF WINTER..54
RESURRECTION..71
THE HONORS OF SERVICE.............................90
THEATER TAKES A HOLIDAY........................106
RETIRING EDWINA..124

SPIRITUAL HYPOCHONDRIA

Written by

David Walling

Copyright (c) 2015

CAST

FATHER MALONE: A kind, good natured priest who sometimes has an exasperating calling.

MARGARET: Father Malone's delightful Irish or Scottish secretary.

CINDY AGANEU: One of Father Malone's parishioners who is WAY over the top in anything she does. Even when confessing.

INT. FATHER MALONE'S OFFICE - DAY

We find Father Malone at his desk when his secretary walks in.

                MARGARET
Father Malone, Cindy Aganeu is outside the office waiting for you.

                FATHER MALONE
                (Panicked)
Is it that time of day already??? Margaret tell her I'm not here, PLEASE!!!

                MARGARET
Father Malone! You want me to lie?

                FATHER MALONE
I'll absolve you!

                MARGARET
                (tsking)
Look at you, taking a deal from the Devil.

                FATHER MALONE
                (head bowed and speaking quietly)
It seems like such a good deal.

                MARGARET
HA! You're the one that was called to become a priest, laddie. So, as they say, you have made your bed and now you have to lie in it. (She pauses

thoughtfully then smiles wickedly.) Just keep poor Cindy out of it.

> FATHER MALONE

MARGARET!!!
> (pause)

You're enjoying this aren't you?

> MARGARET
> (laughing)

Aye. I do sometimes enjoy it when the truly righteous get a bit of humbling.

> FATHER MALONE
> (as Margaret is leaving)

I'm pretty sure that's a sin, Margaret! I'll be expecting you at confession!!

> MARGARET
> (Still laughing)

I'll be there, Father. I'll be there. Go on in, Cindy, the Father will see you now.

> CINDY

Thank you, Margaret

Cindy walks in and holds her hand out to Father Malone. He takes it and shakes it.

CINDY (cont'd)
Oh Father! It is so good to see you!

FATHER MALONE
Hello Cindy. How are you today?

CINDY
(Collapsing in a chair)
Oh Father. I am so glad we have these counseling sessions. I am such a TERRIBLE person! I'm going to Hell, Father.

FATHER MALONE
Now Cindy. I can't believe that of you.

CINDY
But it's True, Father! Why just 45 minutes ago I was a glutton!!

FATHER MALONE
Cindy. You are as skinny as a rail? How can you be a glutton and be so thin?

CINDY
(wailing)
I had a saltine cracker with my soup, Father!

FATHER MALONE
A saltine cracker, Cindy? Really?

CINDY
Children in Africa probably don't even get crackers, Father. They might not even get proper soup and I had BOTH! I'm going to Hell, Father. I'm sure of it.

FATHER MALONE
I doubt you are going to Hell, Cin...

CINDY
It's a deadly sin, Father. DEADLY!!!

FATHER MALONE
Well, that is true. How about three hail Marys and...

CINDY
Oh I am not near done, Father.

FATHER MALONE
(with a sigh)
Go on.

CINDY
I also committed the sin of GREED, Father!

FATHER MALONE
Greed?

CINDY
Yes, Father! Another deadly sin! I took TWO crackers! I have the other one in my purse! I am so going to Hell.

FATHER MALONE
Damn those saltine crackers!!

CINDY
I know, right? And that's not the worst. Envy, Father! I was ENVIOUS!

FATHER MALONE
(curious)
Of a few crackers?

CINDY
No no. I was with my friend, Debbie. You see, Father. I had saltine crackers and Debbie had Swedish Boolie Wafer Crackers.

WONDERFUL DELICIOUS BOOLIE WAFER CRACKERS, FATHER!!!

FATHER MALONE
(wide eyed little fear of crazy Cindy) Boolie Wafer Crackers?

CINDY
YES!!! Oh I wanted those Wafer Crackers, Father. I wanted them REAL BAD. Now we aren't friends anymore.

FATHER MALONE
You aren't friends because you wanted her Boolie Wafer Crackers?

CINDY
Oh no, Father. Because she made me sin.

FATHER MALONE
(putting his face in his hands) How did she do that?

CINDY
Well, I was so upset because of the envy that I told her I just wanted to go home and sleep the rest of the day. Do you know what she said, Father? Do you????

FATHER MALONE
How could I? Maybe you should tell me.

CINDY
She said that seemed a bit slothful!! Can you believe that, Father? A girl wants a little rest and it's called SLOTHFUL!!!

FATHER MALONE
I can see how it might be construed as slothful but...

CINDY
(as if he hadn't started talking)
It made me mad, Father. It made me SOOOO MAD that I keyed her car. Do you know what that's called???

FATHER MALONE
A felony?

CINDY

Wrath, Father. It was HORRIBLE! To make matters worse, as I was leaving, I ran into the delivery man for the restaurant! He was carrying a case of Swedish Wafer Crackers, Father. WAFER CRACKERS, Father!! SWEDISH BOOLIE WAFER CRACKERS!!! Well after all that had happened I just... Just....WANTED HIM. I wanted to throw him on the ground and ravish him and his mouth watering wafer crackers, Father.

Cindy collapses back in the chair panting.

FATHER MALONE
(fanning his face with his hand)
And?

CINDY
(as if the whole thing she just went through was nothing) Nothing. That's all I have, Father.

FATHER MALONE
(still fanning his face)
Well, that's good.

FATHER MALONE (cont'd)
(muttering under his breath) That's more than enough.

CINDY
What?

                    FATHER MALONE
Oh, Nothing.

                    CINDY
So what's my penance, Father?

                    FATHER MALONE
How about four Hail Mary's and an Act of Contrition? Sound good?

                    CINDY
              (getting up and ready to leave)
That sounds wonderful, Father. Thank you.

                    FATHER MALONE
You are welcome. I do have a question, though.

                    CINDY
              (pausing)
Yes, Father?

                    FATHER MALONE
Why do you schedule these sessions to confess rather than go to the confessional?

                    CINDY
              (horrified)
Somebody might see me!!!!

FATHER MALONE
So? A lot of people go to confession. Most in the Church, actually.

CINDY
(said with disdain and disgust as she stomps away) I don't know about those other people, Father, but I do, after all, have my Pride!!!

LIKE A SOFT WIND

Written by

David Walling

Copyright (c) 2014

CHARACTERS

CLAUDIA: A lovely older lady around 80 who is staying at an assisted-living facility.

GIRL ONE: A very young Laurie

GIRL TWO: A very young Claudia

MIDDLE AGED CLAUDIA: Married and has kids. Around 50 or so.

ALVIN: Claudia's Husband. Around 45 or so.

CLAUDIA DAUGHTER: In this she's a heartbroken sister.

LAURIE: Claudia's best friend through the ages.

NURSE: A nurse in training. Is young and just starting off in her field.

JENNET: A middle aged RN working her shift this evening.

VOICE FROM THE BACK: The voice of the director of a play. Can be woman or man. He/She is conducting auditions.

INT. ROOM DAY

A woman walks through the door dressed in black. She is carrying a purse with a tissue clutched in her hand. She sniffles as she comes in. She turns, shuts the door and leans against it for a moment letting out a small sob. She visibly chokes it back and proceeds into the room where there are boxes stacked up waiting next to a desk (made of boxes) for her.

CLAUDIA
Oh Laurie, why? Why did you have to go before me? You were the last one to know me as the girl I am...

She looks at her hands and fiddles with her dress while looking at herself up and down.

CLAUDIA
...not this person I look like.

She sits at the "desk". Wipes her eyes and looks over at the stack of boxes scowling slightly. She suddenly looks up kind of angry and shakes her fist at the sky.

CLAUDIA (cont'd)
And you left me with your shit like you said you would, you vengeful ol' bitch!

She lowers her hand and looks down and wipes her eyes.

CLAUDIA (cont'd)
You lovely vengeful ol' bitch.

She abruptly pulls herself together. Shakes her head in denial and slams her tissue onto the desk.

>   CLAUDIA (cont'd)
>   No. Not any more today. No.

She reaches over and gets ready to drag box number one over to her, pauses, then grabs box number two.

>   CLAUDIA (cont'd)
>   I am NOT doing it in the order YOU want me to,
>   Laurie. You control freak. Now, let's see what you
>   left me.

She looks up to the sky again.

>   CLAUDIA (cont'd)
>   And it better not be anything from that Duck Dynasty
>   taxidermy hobby of yours or I am going to find a
>   medium to put your soul in the same grave as your
>   husband Earl! I told you two not to try anything from
>   that Kama Sutra book.

She rummages through a second and pulls out a rag doll.

>   CLAUDIA (cont'd)
>   Oh, Laurie. This is from when we first met. We
>   became the best of friends.

LIGHT COMES UP ON TWO LITTLE GIRLS FIGHTING OVER A DOLL.

FIRST GIRL
It's MY DOLL now GIVE IT BACK!

SECOND GIRL
Your MOM said to SHARE!!!

FIRST GIRL
So?? It's STILL my DOLL now LET GO!

SECOND GIRL
NO!

FIRST GIRL
YES!

SECOND GIRL
NO!

They both scream and when the head tears off the body they both stop screaming and stare.

SECOND GIRL
Cool. A zombie.

FIRST GIRL
I want the head.

SECOND GIRL
I already have the head.

Second girl starts running off and first girl follows.

                    FIRST GIRL
        You can have the body! It's STILL mine!

                    CLAUDIA
        Oh Laurie, those were the days. I am so glad you
        kept this. I guess I was wrong when I said you were a
        sentimental old fool for keeping these things.

There is a pause while she contemplates the doll. She suddenly
tosses it back in the box.

                    CLAUDIA
        Nope. I wasn't. Let's see what else you left.

Rummages some more and comes up with a newspaper clipping.

                    CLAUDIA (cont'd)
        Wow. You kept the obituary.

She softly chokes back a sob.

                    CLAUDIA (cont'd)
        I think that was when I noticed how lonely it could
        get. I think that was the time when it started. It was
        bad enough that Zach was 18 and we got the news.

LIGHT COMES UP ON A MARINE STANDING IN DRESS
BLUES TALKING TO TWO PEOPLE AND A TEENAGE GIRL.

                    MIDDLE AGED CLAUDIA
        NO!

> ALVIN
> ZACH!

Girl runs away crying.

> ALVIN
> What happened?

> MIDDLE AGED CLAUDIA
> (starts to cry)

The people talk silently as the light fades out on them and recent Claudia continues.

> CLAUDIA (cont'd)
> They said he was brave. They said he saved a lot of men's lives and that he was a hero. I didn't care. I didn't care at all. My baby was gone and then...

Alvin, holding his wife and sobbing himself suddenly grabs his chest and falls to the floor. We hear the sound of an ambulance coming.

> CLAUDIA
> Poor Alvin just couldn't take it. He was only 38. It's not right losing a son. It's not right. It's worse when you lose a son and a husband on the same day. People came to the funeral and for a while they were there, damn near up my ass at times. But it stopped. It slowly faded away. I found that the friends I had that were married rarely invited me over anymore. I think they were uncomfortable and didn't want to

shove their relationship in my face. Or they just didn't know what to say. My friends who had children were very similar. It was almost like if they visited with me their children would be in danger. It wasn't always fair but I survived. I still had Alyssa. Her and I could conquer the world together. A lot of her friends treated her the same way. They were uncomfortable and faded into the background. Alyssa never really got over that I don't think. You, though Laurie, never stopped being my friend. You were my saving grace. When the world started getting lonely, there you were, through it all. You be sure to tell Zach and Alvin I said hello and I miss them.

She puts the clipping away and drags over another box. She scrounges around for a min and comes up with a picture frame with her picture in it.

                  CLAUDIA (cont'd)
OH MY GOODNESS!! My first play!! I remember you making me go and try out for the part. Right after Alyssa went to college. I was still working at the factory and I remember you telling me I was being too reclusive. You were bound and determined to bring me "out of my shell". It was the single most scary thing I had ever done. And one of the best. There weren't too many entertainment options for a middle aged single mother of a college graduate to do. It took a lot to put her in college. You were right, though. I was too much alone. Can't blame Alyssa though. Working on her PHD took up a LOT of time

and she had met her now husband and they were totally engrossed with each other. It's only natural I would get pushed aside a bit. The theater was just the thing I needed. That first audition, though. WHEW.

LIGHT COMES UP ON A MIDDLE-AGED LADY LOOKING OUT INTO THE AUDITORIUM.

                MIDDLE AGED CLAUDIA
Hello?

                VOICE FROM THE BACK
Go ahead. Which song did you pick?

                MIDDLE AGED CLAUDIA
Song?

                VOICE FROM THE BACK
Yes. Didn't you know you were auditioning for a musical?

                MIDDLE AGED CLAUDIA
OH NO! Sorry! I didn't prepare for a song. What do I have to sing?

                VOICE FROM THE BACK
They are all original pieces. You won't know them. How about you just sing "Mary Had a Little Lamb".

                MIDDLE AGED CLAUDIA
Mary had a little lamb?

VOICE FROM THE BACK
Yes. You DO know it, yes?

MIDDLE AGED CLAUDIA
(flustered)
Yes.

VOICE FROM THE BACK
Then we are waiting.

She starts singing Mary Had a Little Lamb very very badly. There is a moment of quiet after she's done.

VOICE FROM THE BACK
Miss...

MIDDLE AGED CLAUDIA
Tandy

VOICE FROM THE BACK
Miss Tandy. We are going to make you a star!

MIDDLE AGED CLAUDIA
REALLY?

VOICE FROM THE BACK
Yes, really.

The light fades out and Claudia starts speaking again.

CLAUDIA

They did too. During the children's scene of the play I was a big overstuffed star. It was a beginning, though, and it gave me something to do and I wasn't near as lonely anymore. You always knew what to say and what to make me do.

Claudia looks up at the sky again.

CLAUDIA

You bossy ol' cow!

She puts away the picture.

CLAUDIA (cont'd)

I wish it could have lasted longer. Alyssa and her husband James moved away to England. I got to see them every other year at Christmas, which was nice. They had two wonderful children. Zach and Ryan. They were a handful but absolutely wonderful. I didn't get to see them much and, for some odd reason, the years seemed to pass by quickly. I think I was 62 when I fell and broke my hip. Alyssa came to help me while I recovered, and we decided it was probably best if I went to a retirement home so that if something like that happened again I wouldn't lay there for five hours waiting for the mailman to arrive. Oh Laurie. You were a good friend. Came every chance you got and we would go out and have meals and talk. You have no idea how precious that was to me. I don't think I ever expressed it properly. The theater seemed to dry up as I got older. Not because I backed off but because there are no parts for people our age. I never told you that because I wanted you to keep going and I know you. You would have stopped out of loyalty. The friends I had there well, some still keep in touch, faded for the most part. The young people coming in don't look much past their parts. I used to go sit in the third row and watch them rehearse. It's a lonely existence when you realize that there is little to no place for you. Somehow, through the years, I became invisible to people. They no longer had more than a passing glance or an invested interest.

She looks up at the sky again and picks up the hanky and dabs her eyes.

CLAUDIA (cont'd)
You always kept my loneliness bearable, Laurie. Thank you for that. Thank you for everything. I miss you so very much. I don't know what I'm doing to do now. Without you here this loneliness has crept up on me slowly. Like a soft wind quietly blowing me away piece by piece and I didn't know how much until you were gone.

There is a knock at the door.

CLAUDIA (cont'd)
Come in.

A nurse walks in.

                NURSE
How are you doing today Claudia?

                CLAUDIA
As well as can be expected, I suppose.

                NURSE
(taking Claudia's blood pressure and pulse) Sitting Shiva for your friend? I see you are sitting on a box and have a few other boxes. Expecting friends over?

                CLAUDIA
Yes, sitting Shiva. No, not anymore.

The Nurse pats her on the hand, smiles at her.

                NURSE
Jennet will be in shortly with your meds, Mrs. Claudia.

Nurse Leaves

                CLAUDIA
Yea, Laurie. I miss you so much.

Her head lowers and she wipes tears from her eyes. Suddenly a lady walks in.

LAURIE
Claudia, Honey.

CLAUDIA
(looking up, her face lighting up with joy.) OH MY GOD! IT'S YOU!!!

Claudia gets up and rushes into the other woman's embrace.

LAURIE
Oh my dear!

The lights go out.

JENNET
Hi Mrs. Claudia. Mrs. Claudia!!!!! CODE BLUE!! CODE BLUE!! GET THE CRASH CART!!!

27

KIDNAPPED

Written by

David Walling

Copyright (c) 2016

CAST

DAN: Martial Arts Instructor.

ANDREW: Young man about 16. Son of Carl and Donna

CARL: Andrew's Dad. Around 40

DONNA: Andrews Mom. Also around 40

STRANGE MAN: Seems to be a nice man who turns scary. He is between 30 and 50. In pretty good shape.

INT. MARTIAL ARTS STUDIO - DAY

We see a teacher and his student practicing martial arts moves. The student seems to be doing a very poor job.

> DAN
>
> C'mon Andrew! You've been at this how long? Are you even practicing?

> ANDREW
>
> Yes, I'm practicing.

> DAN
>
> Then why are you so bad at this? You should have improved at least a little bit in the last month.

> ANDREW
>
> I'll try harder, I swear.

> DAN
> (shaking his head)
> I am not sure you are suited to this. Not everyone is.

> ANDREW
>
> I will do better. I will! I am just not coordinated. I'll practice more.

                    DAN
            (looking out the window)
        We'll see. Your dad is here. Clean up and get your
        stuff together while I go talk to him.

Andrew does a single perfect kick then sighs after his teacher had gone out the door to speak to his father. He then starts picking up his stuff and putting it in his gym bag.

INT. HOUSE - LATER

Carl and Andrew walk into the house and Carl throws his keys on a small table by the door.

                    CARL
        Honey, we're home!

                    DONNA
        (coming in from another room) Hi dear. (She gives
        him a big hug) How are my two favorite men today?
        (She leans over and gives her son a kiss on the
        forehead.

                    ANDREW
        MOOOM!!

                    DONNA
        Live with it. In a few more years you'll go off to
        college and I won't get to do it anymore. Well, Dear?

CARL
(He swings her around and gives her a kiss) My day was wonderful, darling.

ANDREW
EWWWW! NASTY!

His parents smile at him as he heads off to another room. When he is out of sight Carl draws away from Donna a bit and looks worried.

CARL
I had a talk with Dan today about Andrews continued training there.

DONNA
Oh? Is he leaving or something?

CARL
No, no. He says that Andrew isn't improving like he should. Is he practicing?

DONNA
Every day. I'll admit some days seem better than others, but he doesn't seem to be doing too badly.

CARL
Well Dan thinks he either isn't suited for it or isn't putting as much effort as he should be. He wanted me to know so that I could decide whether to keep spending money on it or not.

DONNA
Hmm. I know he's been practicing hard. Every day after school like clockwork. When he sees me watching, though, he does get a bit shy and waits for me to leave. Do you think it's just him being shy?

We start hearing faint but horribly off key singing in the background.

CARL
I don't know. Since he IS practicing then let's keep his lessons going a bit longer.

DONNA
I think that would be a good idea. Maybe talk to him about it.

CARL
I kinda did in the car. He said he would do better. I'll give him a chance for it. Sooo. How was your day?

DONNA
EXCELLENT! Picked up mom today and we went to the farmer's market. Dinner is going to be GREAT! So wash up and we'll eat. Oh, and be mindful of using the cold water. I can hear Andrew already in the shower.

CARL
OMG that singing! Poor boy couldn't carry a tune if it was strapped to him with duct tape.

                    DONNA
              (wincing at a few notes)
            Now now. At least he tries.

                    CARL
            He does at that.

INT. HOUSE - LATER

We see Andrews parents coated up and ready to go out and Andrew enters the room.

                    CARL
            Drew we are going...

                    ANDREW
            Yeah yeah. It's date night. You can keep your grossness to yourself.

                    CARL
              (laughing)
            We'll be back about 10.

                    ANDREW
            Ok. Can I go over to Evan's?

                    DONNA
            Did you do your homework?

ANDREW
Lady, when do I NOT do my homework?

DONNA
(smiling)
One hopes that you will be SOMEWHAT of a normal 14 year old kid.

ANDREW
That would be boring.

DONNA
(giving him a hug)
You can go. Well, as long as your father has no objections.

CARL
None what so ever. Have a good time.

They wave and leave. Andrew immediately gets on his cell.

ANDREW
Evan? It's me. Hey, I am going to go to the park. I told my parents I was going over to your house. If they call can you cover for me? What? Oh. Play a little basketball. Just wander around a bit. I need some time to myself. Yes, I am alone now but it's INSIDE. I want some fresh air. Soo? I'll wear bright clothes. I'll be fine. Will you cover? Ok, thanks. Cost me what? NO! You know I'm not giving up any of MY comics.

How about I just buy you the new issue that's coming out next week? Good. It's a deal. Thanks, man.   Bye.

Andrew hangs up, puts his phone in his pocket, grabs his basketball and leaves the house.

EXT. PARK - EVENING

We find Andrew bouncing a basketball against a wall. After a min or two we see an older guy dragging a footlocker behind him. He drags it close and then sits down on it panting and pulling out a rag to wipe his brow.

                     STRANGE MAN
Hey Kid.

                     ANDREW
(turning around and keeping his eyes cast downward)
Me, sir?

                     STRANGE MAN
Yea. What you doing out here alone and so late? Ain't ya got no family?

                     ANDREW
Yes sir. But they aren't home right now.

                     STRANGE MAN
So you snuck out, did ya?

Andrew just stares at the ground and doesn't answer.

                    STRANGE MAN (cont'd)
                    (with a knowing grunt)
Don't you know it's dangerous out here this late at night?

                    ANDREW
                    (glancing up at him)
Dangerous?

                    STRANGE MAN
Yeah, dangerous. There are drug dealers and junkies and all kinds of perverts out here after dark.

                    ANDREW
I'm just playing basketball.

                    STRANGE MAN
Doesn't matter. Do you think they care about that? Someone could hit you over the head and drag out outta here and nobody would be the wiser. Do you want that to happen?

Andrew doesn't answer

                    STRANGE MAN (cont'd)
Well, do you?

                    ANDREW
No, sir.

STRANGE MAN
Then get your ass home where it's safe and don't be stupid next time.

ANDREW
Yes, sir.

STRANGE MAN
(just as Andrew starts to leave) Wait a second, kid.

ANDREW
(turning)
Yes, sir?

STRANGE MAN
Tell you what. You help me take this footlocker to my car and I'll give you a ride home.

ANDREW
You sure, sure? It's not very far.

STRANGE MAN
Sure, I'm sure. I'd feel bad leaving you out here with the screwed-up freaks that hang out here. Plus, you'd be helping me.

ANDREW
Ok.

STRANGE MAN
(smiling)
Great. Here, grab that other end.

They carry the footlocker offstage. We hear keys and a trunk open.

STRANGE MAN (cont'd)
Careful now! Don't bang it! Good. Push it all the way to the back. Further. All the way. Yes. All the way.

ANDREW
It's all the...HEY!!

We hear a trunk slam.

ANDREW (cont'd)
LET ME OUT! LET ME OUT! HELP!

A car door opens then slams shut and we hear a car peel away in a squeal of tires.

INT. BASEMENT - LATER

We see the strange man dragging Andrew by the throat into the room.

STRANGE MAN
Stop struggling you little bastard! You are just making things worse for yourself!

He sets Andrew on his feet and faces him. Hits him in the jaw, leaving Andrew dazed and flings him into a chair.

> STRANGE MAN (cont'd)
> Now you little stupid shit. You're going to get what stupid little kids deserve.

> ANDREW
> But why? Why, Mister?

> STRANGE MAN

> Why? Because I want to. You little fancy kids with your fancy clothes think you're better than anyone else. Well you're not. I grew up without anything. When I wanted more, my father made sure I learned my lesson and was humble. Just like your smug ass is going to get.

> ANDREW
> Please! Please let me go. I promise I won't tell anyone. You can keep my ball.

> STRANGE MAN
> (backhands him)
> Do you think I'm stupid, kid? The difference between me and my father is that I learned. I learned not to keep people around who can tell on me.

> ANDREW
> Y-you're going to k-k-kill me sir?

                    STRANGE MAN
           (smiling and in a quieter voice) You're damn right,
           kid. Right after I'm done taking all I can get from
           you.   Go ahead and scream, kid. This is a farm. There
           ain't nobody for miles around.

The lights go out. After a few seconds we hear a struggle and the lights come back up with Andrew standing over a body wiping his knife on his pant leg.

                       ANDREW
              (quietly and with a smile)
           Four down, three to go.

FADE TO BLACK

IT'S NOT YOU

Written by

David Walling

Copyright (c) 2016

CAST

CLOWN: Charlie's Dad. He's around 40 to 50. He's a child abuser. Real violent and nasty.

CHARLIE: A young man about 16 or 17. He's quiet and very well liked by all the staff and teachers at his school.

KEN: Between 16 and 18. Ken is a bully. He has a small group of people who hang around with him most of the time. He bullies Charlie on a regular basis.

JULIE: Ken's girlfriend. She loves seeing Ken fight over her. She is very self-centered and an all around horrid person.

OFFICER PHIL: An officer that works security at the door of the school. He has known Charlie for a LONG time and thinks the world of him.

NARRATOR: The guy, or gal, off scene giving valuable information to the audience.

INT. IN A HOME - NIGHT

We hear the keys trying to open a lock. There is a bit of fumbling then the key opens it and the door opens. In walks a man in a clown outfit with a bottle of booze. He's obviously drunk and stumbling.

CLOWN
Charlie. CHARLIE!!!

A young teen comes out of the bedroom. He had obviously been sleeping and is wearing a t-shirt and sleep pants.

CHARLIE
What?

CLOWN
Where the hell were you?

CHARLIE
I was in bed asleep.

CLOWN
And you couldn't come open the door for your old man? What the hell?

CHARLIE
I was asleep. I didn't hear you.

The man stumbles over to Charlie and grabs him by the shirt.

CLOWN
Where's my dinner? Huh? Where's my damn dinner?

CHARLIE
(trying to cower)
It's in the microwave.

CLOWN
In the microwave? In the MICROWAVE?

The man rushes him and slams Charlie into the wall.

CLOWN (cont'd)
I work all day entertaining other people's brats just so we can have food on the table and you have it in the microwave?

CHARLIE
(panicked and jabbering)
I'm sorry! I'm sorry!

CLOWN
You're damn right your sorry!

The clown hits Charlie and, still holding onto his shirt with one hand, follows him to the ground hitting with every word.

CLOWN (cont'd)
Next. Time. Have. It. On. The. Table!

The man suddenly stands up.

                    CLOWN (cont'd)
               Do you understand me?

                    CHARLIE
                    (whimpering)
          Y-yes.

                    CLOWN
Good. Now get it on the table while I wash off my
hand.

                    CLOWN (cont'd)
(he kicks Charlie once and starts walking away) You
got blood all over me.

EXT. SCHOOL - DAY

We see Charlie get off the bus. His head is down and he is trying to
quickly walk to the doors of the school. A group of jocks and some
of their girlfriends are outside and notice him.

                    KEN
          Wilson!

Charlie ignores him and tries to walk faster. Ken runs up and grabs
him by the backpack and swings him around and all but drags him to
the group.

KEN (cont'd)
Where ya going, Wilson? We have a question for you.

CHARLIE
Not today, Ken. Please leave me alone today.

KEN
(talking to the others in the group) What do you think fellas, and ladies? He already looks a little beat up. Should we give him a break today?

CROWD
(they ring out with a chorus of hell no's and other such sentiments. Hell no! No way! Not a chance! etc)

KEN
The people have spoken. Sorry, Charlie. We all have to have our daily enjoyments. Speaking of enjoyments don't you think Julie here is pretty?

Charlie glances at Julie but stays quiet.

KEN (cont'd)
Well don't you or are you a fag?

Charlie still stays silent.

JULIE
Oh my god. Are you going to let him disrespect me like that?

KEN

(grabbing Charlie with both hands by his shirt) Your faggot ass thinks she's ugly?

CHARLIE

No!

KEN

Oh, you think she's pretty now? C'mon. Tell her she's pretty.

CHARLIE

You're pretty.

KEN

(glancing over Charlie's shoulder and lets him go) That's better. Don't ever disrespect her again. You're getting off easy today because Coach Harlow is coming over here. Before you go, tell me again why you keep getting this trouble from us?

CHARLIE

It's not you, it's me.

KEN

That's right. You should have been a different person. Now shoo.

Charlie hurries off to the school.

INT. SECURITY LINE IN SCHOOL - CONTINUOUS

Charlie sets his backpack and belt on the conveyor belt and steps through the machine. It beeps.

> OFFICER PHIL
> Heya Charlie, come on over so we can use the wand. I saw you put your belt through the x-ray so at least we know it's not one of your huge belt buckles this time.

Charlie walks over to the officer and before he uses the wand he beckons to him, so he can whisper to him. The officer leans in.

> OFFICER PHIL (cont'd)
> Yes?

> CHARLIE
> I have a prince Albert now.

> OFFICER PHIL
> What?

> CHARLIE
> I have a prince Albert.

> OFFICER PHIL
> You got your dick pierced?

                    CHARLIE
                    (nodding)
          Twice. Do you want to see?

                  OFFICER PHIL
          Holy... Wow. You're a braver kid than I ever was.
          Naa. Grab your bag and get out of here.

                    CHARLIE
          Thanks. Have a good day.

                  OFFICER PHIL
          You too.

INT. BATHROOM - LATER

We find Charlie looking in a mirror that's broken but still on the wall. He's breathing heavy and is sweating. He stares for a bit. Nods to the image in the mirror and takes off down the hall.

INT. CLASSROOM - MOMENTS LATER

Charlie walks into the class room, reaches into his pants and pulls out a snub-nosed pistol from his pair of underwear holster. He shoots three of the guys from the group. 2 in the head and one in the chest twice. Then he walks over to Ken who is trying to cower under a desk.

KEN
Oh my God, Oh my God. Please! Please, Charlie. I'm sorry. I'm SORRY!!!!

CHARLIE
No need to be sorry Ken. Not at all. You see, it's not you, it's me.

BANG!

FADE TO BLACK

We hear sirens and someone saying, "he was a straight A student".

NARRATOR
If you have a friend like Charlie that is in a similar home situation or a friend that is getting bullied. Tell someone. Don't let tragedy be your wakeup call.

OUT OF WINTER

Written by

David Walling

Copyright (c) 2016

CAST

HARRISON: A man in his late 30's early 40's who is grief-stricken.

MAN 1: Man who hollers out in the background.

GARY: A man in is mid-twenties to his early thirties. Pretty athletic.

GIRLFRIEND: Gary's girlfriend.

ESMERELDA: A widowed lady who understands grief and has been sent to deliver a letter.

LEANNE (VOICE): A teenager's voice. She is Harrison's daughter who knew she was going to die and set up a letter for him… and a date.

EXT. CITY STREET - NIGHT

We hear an exchange of happy new years off in the distance then you here one close up. In stumbles and obviously drunk man brown bagging it.

                    HARRISON
          Happy New Year? HAPPY NEW YEAR???? Screw you!!!

                    MAN 1
               (in the background)
          Screw you too!! Bastard!!

Man stumbles a bit then pauses. He takes a couple swigs, looks up and starts shaking his fist at the sky.

                    HARRISON
          You did this! You made me love then you snatched her away! How many more times are you going to do it? How much do you think I can take! I loved her so much! Were you jealous? Don't you have enough, or do you just want to see me miserable! Well? Here I am! Miserable! Are you happy?

Harrison bends his head and wobbles and sobs quietly for a min before he looks up again.

HARRISON
Why? Why would you take her? She had so much love to give! She was full of life! She brought smiles to everyone who encountered her! Why? She deserved so much more time! The world needed her. She was a light in the dark!

HARRISON (cont'd)
Don't you two look happy.

Gary
Yes. Yes we are.

HARRISON
It's not going to last.

Gary
(pausing and turning to face him) What?

HARRISON
I said, asshole, that it's not going to last.

Gary
(turning around at the tugging of his girlfriend) You're drunk and don't know what you are talking about.

HARRISON
(Jumping in front of the guy) I do! She'll leave you and will rip your heart out on the way! They all leave and you just end up broken and bleeding.

Gary
(shoving Harrison out of the way) Back off, you old drunk before I beat the crap out of you.

HARRISON
(setting his bottle down before putting up his fists) Oh. Ok. So, you think you can hurt me, tough guy? You can't hurt me! C'mon. Bring it... Bitch!

Gary
(pulling away from his girlfriend) You got it, old man.

GIRLFRIEND
No, Gary, just leave it alone. Lets go.

GARY
(turning to his girlfriend) No. I'm going to teach this guy a lesson.

GIRLFRIEND
Please! He's just old and drunk Let's go.

GARY
I don't think...

Harrison hits Gary in the back of the head

HARRISON
(eyes widening in challenge) Oh! Oh! Did that get your attention? How about I give you a baby one.

Harrison swings really slow and barely taps Gary.

HARRISON
(eyes widening in near delight) Oh ho!! Did that hurt... Ya wussie!!

GIRLFRIEND
Gary, lets GO!

HARRISON
Yeah. Let her go, GAAAARY. She's just going to leave you anyway. They all do. Missy, go find you a real man.

GARY
(drawing back his fist and hitting Harrison knocking him on his butt) You son of a...

HARRISON
OW!! I'm old! What's wrong with you?

GARY
You hit me in the back of the head!

HARRISON
So? I'm drunk and I'm old! I wasn't ready!

GARY
Get up then, you old drunk!

GIRLFRIEND
                OMG GARY!!! Come on!

The girlfriend grabs Gary's arm and drags him away.

                    HARRISON
                It will end in heartache! I warn you!! Ow.

Harrison gets up rubbing his jaw and mumbling to himself. He gets his bottle and walks over to a park bench and sits down next to the statue there. He looks at the statue and starts talking.

                    HARRISON
                (raising his bottle to the statue) She was beautiful,
                you know. The most beautiful girl in the world. Her
                hair was as dark as midnight. A midnight that was full
                of life. Her eyes birthed stars and cast them out to the
                night sky. When your soul weighed heavy with
                demons known and unknown, she would smile. All
                the dark places would be filled with light. A joy so
                rich as to be like the gentle song of Angels upon the
                breeze. If she shed a tear it was the purest heartbreak
                you ever saw and it would bring out compassion from
                the hardest of hearts. She gave freely. She was always
                collecting or making things for those in need. She
                loved so fiercely that she was like a roaring fire that
                would relight the fires of hope in the downtrodden
                and broken. She was a joy to behold.

Harrison takes a few more swigs of his booze. He looks at the statue.

HARRISON (cont'd)
Her laugh. Now don't get me started on her laugh. It was... Well, it was. Oh it was terrible. It was like no laughter you ever heard. It was a guffaw crossed with the snort of a pig and the trumpeting of an elephant. The most horrible and wonderful sound in the universe. And it was always accompanied by a fart. A few of them if she couldn't stop.

Harrison pauses.

HARRISON (cont'd)
I miss her laugh.

Harrison starts to cry and then he takes a couple swigs of his booze and once again looks at the statue.

HARRISON (cont'd)
You're the best listener ever, buddy.

Harrison slaps the statue on the arm then gets wide eyed and does it again.

HARRISON (cont'd)
Holy smokes, man! How long have you been out here? You're frozen solid!

Harrison gets up and stumbles back and forth trying to pace.

HARRISON (cont'd)
What do I do? What do I do?

Harrison pauses, picks up a rock and throws it at the statue. When it bounces off he lets out a big breath.

HARRISON (cont'd)
Yep. Stone dead. Too late for an ambulance. I need to get out of here.

Harrison starts to stumble away when he runs into a lady dressed in a suit.

HARRISON (cont'd)
Excuse me. Par pardon me.

EZMERELDA
Hello. Mr. DeAngelo I am Ezmerelda Stein. I am with Miller, Ansel, Grace and Stein Law Offices.

HARRISON
Law offices?

EZMERELDA
Yes, Mr. DeAngelo.

HARRISON
(looking over his shoulder where the couple had vanished.) Were you standing on a street corner or something? That was FAST. I swear I only hit him with baby taps!

EZMERELDA
I'm not here for... Whatever that is, Mr. DeAngelo. I am here to deliver this letter.

She holds out a letter to Harrison who stares at it blankly.

HARRISON
Is it a subpoena?

EZMERELDA
No. Mr. DeAngelo, it's a letter.

HARRISON
Am I being served?

EZMERELDA
No. Mr. DeAngelo. It is just a letter. We were hired months ago by someone to deliver it here at this place at this time and specifically by me. All I know is it's a letter. The partners will not tell me anything more but I am to stay here until you read it aloud.

HARRISON
At this place? On this day?

EZMERELDA
Yes, Mr. DeAngelo.

HARRISON
HOLY CRAP! Do you belong to the psychic friends network? How did they know I would be here, now?

EZMERELDA
(a little exasperated)
I have no idea, Mr. DeAngelo. It's all very strange to me. Shall we sit?

Harrison and Ezmerelda go and sit on the bench with Ezmerelda sitting in the middle.

HARRISON
(leaning over and looking at the statue then at Ezmerelda) Don't mind him. He's a deep thinker. The quiet type.

EZMERELDA
(stares at the statue for a second then back to Harrison. She pauses a moment then scoots closer to the statue) Uh. Ok.

Harrison opens the envelope and pulls out the letter. He stares at it for a second then seems to half way sober up.

HARRISON
(looking wide eyed at Ezmerelda) It's in her handwriting.

EZMERELDA
Who, Mr. DeAngelo?

HARRISON
(choking back a sob and hugging the letter to his chest) My heart.

EZMERELDA
Oh. (after a few moments she reaches out and tugs on the paper.) Would you like me to read it for you, Mr. DeAngelo?

HARRISON
(nods and hands the letter to Ezmerelda and almost whispers) Please.

As Ezmerelda starts to read it starts off with her voice then there is a voice over that will read the rest.

EZMERELDA LEANNE MERGE
To the greatest man I have ever known...

LEANNE
(said sternly)
Stop wallowing!

HARRISON
(looking at Ezmerelda)
That's a bit harsh.

EZMERELDA
Huh. Indeed.

LEANNE
I am not being mean.

Harrison and Ezmerelda glance at each other and Harrison shrugs.

LEANNE (cont'd)
You've had enough time to be miserable and to live in that misery. It's time to start living again. I am pretty confident I know how your day has gone. First you stayed in bed moping almost all day. Then you went to Ed's Liquor Store and grabbed you a fifth of rum and I am betting most of it is gone.

Harrison scootches his bottle a bit behind him.

LEANNE (cont'd)
I would also bet money that you have been yelling at people and got into a fight.

HARRISON
(looking at Ezmerelda)
I never.

LEANNE
Stop lying.

HARRISON
Ok. That's creepy.

Ezmerelda looks up at Harrison and nods in agreement then goes back to the letter.

LEANNE
It's time to let go of the nonsense, look up at the sky, take in a breath.

Harrison does this. While he is still looking up he starts talking to Ezmerelda.

> HARRISON
> I taught her to dance here. She didn't know how, and she insisted on learning. We danced and danced until she couldn't dance anymore. We came here every year and danced on New Years Eve and watched the fireworks.

> EZMERELDA
> (putting her hand on his arm) Oh Mr. D...

> HARRISON
> Harrison

> EZMERELDA
> Harrison.

> HARRISON
> (patting her hand and smiling at her) I will miss this. Read on, please.

> LEANNE
> Now that you've told Ezmerelda about dancing...

> HARRISON
> Ok. It's freaking me out.

EZMERELDA
(a bit out of breath)
Me too.

LEANNE
There is something you should know about her. She lost her husband a few years back and she lost her son in Iraq last year.

HARRISON
Oh my God.

Ezmerelda holds her hand over her mouth.

EZMERELDA
I want you to dance with her. Dance with her for me. She understands, and she needs someone who understands her. Dance with her. Start your life again. I have never wanted for Love. I have always been cherished. I have always had more than I needed because you are so wonderful. That is why it was always so easy for me to share. Thank you for my good heart. Dance for me. Both of you dance for me. I love you Dad.

EZMERELDA
(gasps)
Dad?

HARRISON
(nods at her)
Oh yes. Not my wife. My daughter. My wife died when she was a baby and it was me and her against the world from that point on. Until she died of cancer at 16.

Harrison cries softly as Ezmerelda hugs and pats him. After a minute we hear a huge clock strike midnight. Ezmerelda suddenly hugs him and cries a bit herself. He pats her and then stands up and holds his hand out.

HARRISON
Shall we bring in the New Year as she requested?

EZMERELDA
(taking his hand and standing up) Wait! There's a bit more.

LEANNE
P.S. I got my driver's license when you weren't looking! P.P.S. Now that I'm dead I bet you wish you had let me go to that concert when I was 14 now, huh?

Harrison laughs a little bit then takes up Ezmerelda and they dance till the lights fade out.

LEANNE VOICE OVER
Happy New year. Have a great new beginning. Love you, Leanne.

RESURRECTION

Written by

David Walling

Copyright (c) 2016

CAST

CARL: A father about 40 to 60. He thinks making a lot of money is the real meaning of success not joining the military. He TRIES to be understanding.

MARY: A Mom who is pretty high strung. She like things neat and orderly.

DAN: Police Chief's son and good friend to the family. Kenneth is one of his best friends.

KENNETH: The son. Is secretly gay. He saw his whole unit killed (many of them his buddies and one was the love of his life. He has flashbacks. PTSD and is somewhat lost.

SARA: Kenneth's sister. She's pretty progressive.

AMANDA: Sara's daughter. She and her Uncle have a really close bond. She's around 10 and has much of innocence about her. She very much loves her Uncle and wants to see him better.

INT. HOUSE - DAY

Before lights come up we hear from one door then the other before they barge in both doors.

CARL
He's not in the garage!

MARY
He's not in the guest house either!

They burst through the doors all dressed up.

CARL
We don't need this today. Not on Easter of all days.

MARY
No kidding. Did you check the diner?

CARL
I checked that first.

MARY
How the hell did he get past the alarms? Did you give him the codes?

CARL
No, Mary, of course not! What kind of moron do you think I am. He WAS in special forces. Maybe getting by alarms is a skill set they have.

MARY

Special Forces. That poor boy. Why did you ever let him go into the military?

CARL

Me? He is a grown man do you think *I* could have ever stopped him when he made a decision? Were YOU ever able to?

MARY

No. I guess not. (she starts to cry) He's destroying our lives. I can't keep doing this. He won't get help. All the help we get him he refuses. I can't live like this! He has to go, Carl.

CARL

Where? Where would he go? Out to the streets? Oh THAT will do a lot of good. We have to give him time, Mary.

MARY

I don't know. I don't care right now. He didn't used to be this way. Is he doing drugs? Is he hanging out with the wrong crowd? Why won't he get help? It's been a YEAR since he came back. He won't keep a job and he won't get help.

CARL

He's been through a lot. He was the only survivor of his group. We just have to find the right way to help him.

MARY

And what until then? Let him destroy our home? Our reputation?

CARL
(anger in his voice)

Reputation? REPUTATION? Our boy's life is on the line and you are worried about our reputation? He was serving our country! You want to just give up on him because your reputation is being called into question? He's seen horrors we can't even imagine. You and I don't even watch scary movies and he's seen one hundred times worse and you want to throw him out because of your reputation?

MARY
(shouting)

What do we do then? Let him destroy our lives because he doesn't want to deal with things? He's ruining everything! I can't take the pressure and the worrying every day that he's going to go off. I can't worry that he's going to get killed anymore. I don't have anything left! I don't know what else to do and I don't have anything left!

CARL
(taking Mary in his arms)

We can do this together. We can. We'll find a way to get through to him.

MARY
How?

CARL
I don't know, exactly, but there has to be a way. Just a bit more time is all I ask. Don't give up on him. That kind, gentle boy we used to know is in there somewhere. Just a little more time.

MARY
Ok. If something doesn't happen soon, Carl, I won't stay. I will go to my mother's.

CARL
Ok. Deal.

There is a knock at the door. Carl and Mary start then she wipes her eyes and straightens herself out while Carl answers the door.

CARL (cont'd)
Dan! This isn't a good time right now.

DAN
(interrupting and walking in) Well make time, Carl. It's about Kenneth.

CARL
(same time as Mary)
You found him?

MARY
(same time as Carl)
Is he ok?

DAN
(Holding up a hand)
Yes, he's asleep in the car and yes, he is ok.

CARL
(relieved)
Passed out?

DAN
No. I don't think so. The bar tender said he only had one drink and was nursing it.

CARL
How did you end up with him?

DAN
There's the rub. I was called after the police had arrived.

MARY
Again????

                    DAN
Yes but I calmed them down. Apparently one of the patrons dropped a beer bottle and something in him snapped and he thought, for a while, that he was in the middle of enemy territory. The bar tender said at one point he screamed like nothing he had ever heard and then passed out on the floor.

                    MARY
            (hand going to mouth)
Oh My God.

                    DAN
Yeah.

                    CARL
Do you think he was reliving that time?

                    DAN
Yeah. How many friends was he with?

                    CARL
Five.

                    DAN
Well he called out 3 names and it was not for anyone there.

                    MARY
Do you have any idea what we should do?

                    DAN
No. He needs to get into into treatment. Do an intervention if you have to. My father may be the chief of police but there is a limit to the leeway we can give.

                    CARL
Thank you, Dan. We'll do that.

                    DAN
You're welcome. Sigh. Now to get him out of my car.

We hear some mumbling and it gets a bit louder. Then a car drives off.

                    KENNETH
(walking in and talking to himself.) I didn't ask for your help.

He stops in surprise at his parents standing there.

                    MARY
                 (tersely)
Go get cleaned up! We are going to mass.

                    KENNETH
I don't want to go to mass.

                    MARY
It's Easter and we are ALL going!

KENNETH
I am NOT going!

CARL
(holding up his hand and stopping Mary's response)
She's right, Kenneth. It's Easter and we should go as a family.

KENNETH
I don't want to go.

CARL
What DO you want? You don't seem to be happy with anything. You don't look for help and any help we find can't do anything because you refuse to talk.

KENNETH
Why would I want to talk? They don't understand. NOBODY understands. They weren't there. They have never been there. They can't help me. All they want to do is poke and prod and stir up shit.

CARL
They HAVE to poke and prod. You don't TALK! They can't help you if you don't talk. What about us? We love you, talk to us!

KENNETH
NO!! I don't want to talk to ANYONE! Don't you understand? You can't HELP!

CARL
Well we can't live like this! You have to talk so you can heal from this.

KENNETH
I. DO. NOT. WANT. TO. TALK. You won't understand! Nobody does!

He starts heading out.

CARL
Where are you going?

KENNETH
To my room to be by MYSELF!

CARL
We are going to mass! We expect you to go with us and we are leaving as soon as your sister gets here!

KENNETH
(out the door already)
Screw Mass!

MARY
(gasping)
See, Carl? He's unreasonable! What are we supposed to do? We can't keep getting him out of trouble and we can't help him. He doesn't want help!

CARL
He does want help but he just doesn't know how to go about it. His friends got blown up right in front of him and one of them shielded his body with his own body.

MARY
I know but it's been a YEAR!!

There is a knock at the door and Carl answers it.

CARL
SARA! AMANDA! (he gives them both a hug)

SARA
Hi Mom, Dad. Listen, Amanda has an idea, for Kenneth, but you need to know about it and I think you need to be open enough to try.

CARL
What? What is it?

SARA
Amanda go see Uncle Kenneth.

MARY
Oh, hon that may not be a good idea. He's in a nasty way today.

AMANDA
He's always nice to me, Grandma. I'll be ok.

                    SARA
            (stopping her mother's protests)
    Let her. She believes she got an answer to a prayer
    and she may have so let her try. It can't hurt.

                    MARY
    What is it.

                    SARA
            (shooing Amanda)
    Go. (she turns back to her mother) Let me tell you a
    story about a big hearted little girl.

Amanda goes out the door, grabs a box and walks back in past her mom and grandparents to Uncle Kenneth's room.

INT. KENNETH'S ROOM - MOMENTS LATER

We find Kenneth hollering at God

                    KENNETH
    What do you want from me? Why
    couldn't you take me too? Is it punishment? Are you
    wanting me to suffer? Don't you care? What DO you
    care about? You know, I am not even sure I believe in
    you anymore? What God could let something like that
    happen to someone who has always tried to be a good
    person for you? How can you exist and let that
    happen?

He collapses in a "chair" and sobs. There is a small knock at the door.

> KENNETH (cont'd)
> GO AWAY!!!

> AMANDA
> (peeking in)
> Uncle Kenneth?

> KENNETH
> (wiping his eyes)
> Oh. It's you, Amanda. Come on in. What can I do you for?

> AMANDA
> (comes in carrying the box) Are you ok?

> KENNETH
> (hugging her)
> I'll be fine. Just having a hard day. How are you.

> AMANDA
> I am good but let me tell you a story.

> KENNETH
> Ok.

> AMANDA
> (staring at him for a second then nodding once) I prayed for you.

KENNETH
You did? How did it go?

AMANDA
Yes, I did now stop interrupting.

KENNETH
(laughs a bit)

AMANDA
I prayed for you. And when I did, Jesus gave me an idea so I went looking and I found him.

KENNETH
(a bit surprised)
You did?

AMANDA
Yes, but he was not at all what I expected. He had tanned skin and spoke with and accent of some kind but he gave me a gift for you.

KENNETH
(glancing at the box)
He did?

AMANDA
Yes. He did. And he told me that I should remind you about today.

KENNETH
What about today?

AMANDA
It is Easter.

KENNETH
(hesitant)
Yes. I think I knew that.

AMANDA
Easter is a time for hope, new beginnings, and rebirth. A resurrection of sorts.

KENNETH
Ok...

AMANDA
Anyway, I was thinking that this will hopefully help you and maybe this will be YOUR resurrection day.

She slides the box over to him and Kenneth opens it up.

KENNETH
OH MY GOD!

AMANDA
Yeah. He's been sleeping and quiet in there the whole time.

KENNETH
(reaching in the box and pulling out a puppy who yips at him) Hi! Are you adorable! You got him for me?

AMANDA
Yes.

KENNETH
(hugging her tight)
Thank you, Amanda. He's wonderful!

AMANDA
(Smiles)
I love you.

KENNETH
(most of his attention on the puppy) I love you too. Oh, my goodness. What should we call you?

Amanda, glancing back before she closes the door, leaves the room. After a few seconds the grandparents and the sister as well as Amanda peek in the door and watch.

KENNETH (cont'd)
Well it IS Easter. Maybe you should be called Egg? Wouldn't that be a hoot? Would you like that? I bet you're a good egg too, aren't you? Yes, you are a good Egg.

Kenneth holds the puppy out and looks at it.

                    KENNETH (cont'd)
                    (hugging the puppy)
            Wow you are a sweet one, aren't you! I have to pick
            up some food and a collar for you. You are perfect.
            You are exactly what Rob...

He pauses then his face becomes a mask of pain for a minute. He hugs the dog again and cries. After a bit he pulls away, looks at the puppy and with a small smile he settles the puppy in his lap.

                    KENNETH (cont'd)
            Let me tell you about five of the best people ever
            created. One who I loved as I have never loved
            before.

Kenneth lets out a sob then gets control of himself.

                    KENNETH (cont'd)
            He would have thought you were perfect. We were
            out patrolling one day, Rob, Lamar, Andy....

Fade to black as he is talking.

THE HONORS OF SERVICE

Written by

David Walling

Copyright (c) 2016

CAST

MR. SPIEGAL: A U.S. Vet who is not able to get the help he needs. He's about 35. He's on the streets now.

SECRETARY: A voice from the V.A. that tells him he is denied care.

GUY: A guy who thinks that all homeless people are on the streets due to laziness.

GUY 2: He is very suspicious of people who are on the streets that claim to be vets.

LADY: A person who's purse is stolen.

GUY 3: A good guy but confused about what the moral thing to do would be.

LEADER OF GROUP: An obviously bad guy.

MSG: The Matchstick Girl. If you don't know about her go read! It's a Christmas story.

Various Ensemble: Part of the leader's gang. Guys girlfriends. Passer by.

NEWS REPORTER: A man or woman who is not seen but voice is heard from off stage when the lights go down.

EXT. ON THE SIDEWALK - EVENING

We open up with hearing someone talking to our main character but not in the same room.

> SECRETARY
> I'm sorry, Mr. Spiegal. The letter declining your claim says it all. We only have your service record and that is what the determination for your disability claim was based on.

> SPIEGAL
> But it's a MEDICAL issue! How can they make a determination based on non- medical records?

> SECRETARY
> It's because that's all they had.

> SPIEGAL
> Because THEY lost them.

> SECRETARY
> Mr. Spiegal, your medical records are your responsibility.

SPIEGAL
How can they be my responsibility if the military made me turn them in??? They were sealed in a packet along with my SRB and handed over when I processed out.

SECRETARY
Are you SURE you don't have them? MY medical records are in my attic safely tucked away.

SPIEGAL
I am POSITIVE. I was made to give them up to the military.

SECRETARY
I'm sorry Mr. Spiegal. You are not eligible for any disability without your supplying records.

SPIEGAL
But I just sai...

SECRETARY
Yes, yes. I know. I'm sorry, I can't help you.

SPIEGAL
But I NEED help.

SECRETARY
If you have another insurance, we could use that.

SPIEGAL
I can't keep a job long enough to get insurance I was hurt, don't you understand? Something is wrong. I need the help.

SECRETARY
I'm sorry. Unless you can provide proof of the damage that was done to you by the military then I can't help you.

SPIEGAL
Don't you see the scars??? I got a silver star and a medal of honor along with a purple heart.

SECRETARY
I'm sure your awards were mentioned in your service records, sir, but there is no proof of the injuries your claim without medical records. So unless you have anything else please step aside for another vet that is waiting.

SPIEGAL
But..

SECRETARY
Do I need to call security?

The lights come up and Mr. Spiegal is sitting on a bench rocking back and forth.

SPIEGAL
54697. 54697. No no. Two dogs. 54697. Ugh. It's crazy talk. What am I thinking of? Crap. I forgot. I am sick of this. I can't keep track of anything.

A couple walks by.

SPIEGAL
Excuse me. Can I please have a dollar or two to help me get a hotel room for the night?

GUY
Get a job you bum. The rest of us don't need hotels because we work for a living.

They hurry past and Spiegal looks saddened and dejected.

SPIEGAL
I don't understand. I just don't understand. What happened? People used to be so kind. Yeah. BEFORE you went crazy. Crazy. I hate it. I HATE IT!!

Spiegal starts to cry.

SPIEGAL
I'm sorry. I'm sorry for whatever I did. Please. I take it all back. Anything I did that was bad I take it back. I'm sorry. Madaline you were the best wife. I am sorry. Boys, I'm sorry. Katie, my only daughter. I'm SORRY!! I'm sorry for whatever this is!

He suddenly stops as if he had never been crying.

> SPIEGAL (cont'd)
> I've got to do something. I have more important things to do. It's cold. Where should I go? By myself. Saturday. Saturday. Saturday? No. It's not Saturday. I have to get out of this cold.

A guy walks by.

> SPIEGAL (cont'd)
> Excuse me, sir. May I have a couple dollars to get a hotel and get out of this cold?

> SPIEGAL (cont'd)
> (to himself)
> What are we doing for Christmas? No not Christmas yet.

The man pauses and looks him up and down.

> GUY 2
> So your sign says you were in the military.

> SPIEGAL
> (a bit nervous)
> Yes sir.

> GUY 2
> What unit were you in?

SPIEGAL
Afghanistan. Afghanistan. Very warm. Lots of sand. Lots of sand. No Christmas. Christmas is coming. Coming soon.

GUY 2
Ok but what unit?

SPIEGAL
Unit?

GUY 2
(loudly and slowly)
YES. WHAT UNIT?

SPIEGAL
5. 5 something. 5 5 5. 5 is May Something.

GUY 2
Yeah. That's what I thought! You disgrace this country by claiming something you never were! You dishonor those men who really served! You disgust me.

The man storms off leaving Spiegal kind of stunned.

SPIEGAL
(shouting after the man)
But I was! I was!

SPIEGAL (cont'd)
(to himself)
The shrapnel. The pain. Burning. Still burning.

He sits back down on the bench.

SPIEGAL (cont'd)
(beats his head with his hands)
Can't remember. Not always. Why? Why?
Madaline! Where is everybody. Damn it's cold.

As he is talking a woman walks by and Spiegal suddenly looks up when she screams because a man steals her purse. Spiegal jumps into action and chases the guy. (they run to the lobby and you hear sounds of a scuffle a couple of movie hits and Spiegal staggers in with the purse in hand. He walks up to an obviously still frightened woman and stiffly offers her the purse.)

LADY
(taking the purse cautiously)
Th-thank you.

SPIEGAL
You're welcome. YOU'RE WELCOME!!

The lady jumps and runs away.

SPIEGAL (cont'd)
You're welcome. You're welcome. Welcome. Warm welcomes. Warm welcomes. Sweating. Sweating and cold are bad. Very bad.

He reaches in his pockets and pulls out a bunch of change and ones. And starts to count.

> SPIEGAL (cont'd)
> One, two, three, four, five. Counting. Counting. Do I have enough? Five. Five. Ok. Six, seven, eight, nine, ten, eleven, twelve, twelve, twelve. Eleven then twelve. Thirteen, fourteen, fifteen, sixteen, seven. Seven seven seven and eighteen. Nineteen twenty, twenty-one, twenty-one. Twenty-two, twenty-three, twenty-four, twenty-five. Five. Five, twenty-five then six, twenty-six. Twenty-seven twenty-eight twenty-nine. Twenty-nine. I have twenty-nine. Need tax. Tax and twenty-nine. Almost enough. Need to be warm.

He puts his money back in his pocket. A few more people walk by and he asks them for money, but they just ignore him.

> SPIEGAL (cont'd)
>
> (as some guy walks by)
> Sir? Sir? Can I please have a couple dollars to get a room for the night?

> GUY 3
> I'm sorry. Are you a vet?

> SPIEGAL
> Yes sir. Yes sir. Yes sir. Yes. From Afghanistan. Afghanistan. Hot, there. So hot.

GUY 3

If I give you money you'll probably just use it for booze or drugs.

SPIEGAL

No. No. No. Don't drink. Don't drink anything but water and soda.

GUY 3

But you do drugs?

SPIEGAL

NO! NO! Don't do drugs. The doctor makes me use drugs and I HATE them I hate them.

GUY 3

Yeah. Right. I don't think I can believe you. It's veteran's day. Have you eaten today?

SPIEGAL

Yes. Ate a lot. A lot at different places.

GUY 3

Well then I am pretty sure you have had enough handouts for today but just in case, here's a dollar. I am pretty sure you can't get any drugs or booze for that so my conscious is clear. Good luck buddy.

SPIEGAL
(as the guy walks off)
Thank you. I don't drink. Don't drink anymore. Makes things bad. Bad. Very bad. Don't drink. Ate today. 1664. No. Not 1664. Need to get out of the cold. So cold. 30. Got thirty. Christmas is coming. How is she today?

Three guys walk up to him and one is the spokesperson.

LEADER OF GROUP
Hey, man, did I hear you say you needed money?

SPIEGAL
Yes. For hotel room. It's cold. Cold. Very cold. 470.

LEADER OF GROUP
I hear you, friend. Well how much do you have?

SPIEGAL
I have thirty. Need thirty-three. Thirty-three for hotel room.

LEADER OF GROUP
(looking around first)
Let us see it and we will give you a 5.

SPIEGAL
No. Put away. You can't see it. I need 4. Just 4.

LEADER OF GROUP
Well we're not giving you an option.

The three guys jump him and beat him up and take all his money and run off. He lays there for a bit then slowly pulls himself back up onto the bench and curls up.

SPIEGAL
Nothing left. Nothing left. So cold. What do I do? Who do I know? 7832. Not numbers. Need ideas. Please help me. Please.

The lights dim and when they come back up a girl walks in and right up to him.

MSG
(shaking him a bit and helping him sit up) Wow. You look cold.

SPIEGAL
I am. Very.

MSG
Well how about we just get you to some place much more comfortable. Come on. Follow me.

SPIEGAL
(looking horrified.)
HELL NO!! I thank you for your kindness, but your parents would have me arrested!

MSG
(laughing)
I haven't lived with my parents for years. I am older than I look.

SPIEGAL
You are?

MSG
Oh yeah. Come on. Let's go.

SPIEGAL
(getting up and following her)
Well, uh. Thanks. What are you doing out on a night like this?

MSG
Helping people.

SPIEGAL
That is very nice of you. Thanks again by the way.

MSG
Glad to do it.

SPIEGAL
Do you live around here?

MSG
I lived here all my life.

SPIEGAL
What do you do? I used to be in the Marine Corps.

MSG
I used to sell match sticks.

The lights go down and we hear a news report.

NEWS REPORTER
We have some breaking news this morning. A war hero was found frozen this morning in Washington Park. Keven Spiegal, a Marine Corps veteran who was credited for saving numerous lives including carrying his commander and five others to safety, was found frozen this morning. He was the recipient of both a silver star and the medal of honor. He received the purple heart when...

THEATER TAKES A HOLIDAY

Written by

David Walling

Copyright (c) 2016

Characters:

LAURA: She's the production manager of this show and she has to have everything perfect and on time. She makes no apologies for her gruff nature. She's the devil. **Immortal**

RICHARD HARPER: One of the actors. He has to die so they, the immortals, can get a vacation. He is obviously gay. **Immortal**

BEANS: Beans does lights and sounds. He's a nice guy but he wants a vacation too. **Immortal**

RACHAEL: She seems to be always playing an angel that directs the dead where to go. She wants a better role. **Immortal**

MARK: GOD

Varied Ensamble: People hanging around doing stuff like building painting and such. They will be there when needing a crowd.

INT. LOCAL COMMUNITY THEATER - EVENING

Lights come down and we hear some hammering.

> LAURA
> C'mon people!! This set isn't going to build itself! We haven't got all day!

Lights come up and Richard comes stomping through the door.

> RICHARD
> I can't believe she sent me in HERE. I wasn't built for this. Hi Beans.

> BEANS
> Hi Richard. So you are the one that got tagged? What did you do to piss her off?

> RICHARD
> She told me to hurry up and I told her I was finding my light and she sent me to you.

> BEANS
> Well Irony of Ironies. I need that light right above you fixed.

> RICHARD
> (looking up)
> I'm pretty sure this is not in my job description. I can't afford to hurt these delicate hands.

BEANS

(staring at him for a moment) What?

RICHARD

(demonstrating)

You know, for waving. You don't think we get these loose wrists without practice, do you? Of course not! Now, what's wrong with this thing? (waving his hands towards the ceiling.)

BEANS

It just needs the light bulb changed. Here.

RICHARD

Don't we have trained professionals to do this? Where's Ashley?

BEANS

(smiling innocently)

In the back room making sure the shows run smoothly by keeping herself from killing all the actors that think she should be doing everything.

RICHARD

(rolls his eyes AND his head then walks over and "picks up" a bulb then drags a box back and stands on it and starts to put the bulb in) I have to get out of here. I am meeting some friends.

Richard starts shaking and making noises and we hear a zapping and the lights flicker on and off then go to black. When they come back up, Richard is standing in a room much like scene one with Rachael standing at a podium.

>   RICHARD
> What, what happened?
>
>   RACHAEL
> You died.
>
>   RICHARD
> What?
>
>   RACHAEL
> Yep. Dead as a door nail.
>
>   RICHARD
> What do you mean?
>
>   RACHAEL
> You are gone, kaput, defunct, slabbed out. You have kicked the bucket. You are deceased.

Richard stares blankly.

>   RACHAEL
>   (sighing)
> The crowds not laughing and you're doing a comedy.

RICHARD
OMG! I'm dead?

RACHAEL
(smiling)
There we go.

RICHARD
What happened? Where is this? It looks like scene one.

RACHAEL
Well, you were electrocuted. You are in the afterlife and it looks like Scene One because that makes most people comfortable. But good news! You are going to be recycled!! Yay!!

RICHARD
No no no. This can't be happening. If I am dead why does this look like Scene One?

RACHAEL
(getting irritated)
If you haven't figured it out yet, Mark is God.

RICHARD
Mark is God? OUR Mark?

RACHAEL
Who else? You heard that phrase that all the world's a stage?

RICHARD
Of course.

RACHAEL
Well it REALLY IS!

RICHARD
And Mark is God?

RACHAEL
Yes. He LOVES the theater.

RICHARD
Mark is God and I am dead. Rachael, why are YOU here?

RACHAEL
(very annoyed)
Typecasting

RICHARD
What?

RACHAEL
Never mind. The fact is, it is time for you to move on.

RICHARD
Wait a minute. This can't be right. Can't you take someone else? What about Meryl Streep?

RACHAEL
HA!! She's not scheduled to die until she's 104.
Maybe she'll have won an Academy Award by then.
She's been on the recycle list for YEARS. The boss
does have his favorites.

RACHAEL
(almost under her breath)
Like Megan. That's why she gets all the good parts.
That bitch.

RICHARD
But I'm too young to die!!

RACHAEL
(under her breath and to herself)
Well you ARE a little early.

Richard
What? Early? What do you mean early?

RACHAEL
You heard that did you? Well doesn't matter. You
need to be moving on to your next destination. Accept
the fact that the life before is no longer available and
move on.

RICHARD
How early am I? Why am I early?

RACHAEL
(frustrated now)
Not early enough now MOVE ON!

BEANS
You better do it, buddy. She's not pleasant when she's agitated.

RICHARD
Beans? What the hell?

RACHAEL
Look. Some of us you met at our little community theater are immortals. We help to keep things running smoothly for our Lord and Master. Beans and I are just two.

RICHARD
Immortals? Wait, you two are immortal and Mark is God and, who's the devil?

RACHAEL
There ISN'T one! And you better move on before you piss us all off!

RICHARD
But you said I was early!

RACHAEL
(with a big sigh)
Look. You were going to die eventually. We just pushed you along a bit because we are TIRED.

RICHARD
Tired?

RACHAEL
Yes, we have been without a day off in over 500 years. WE DESERVE A HOLIDAY!!! We WANT a holiday! The boss promised us that if we fulfill our quota then we can HAVE a holiday and you are the last of our quota!!

RICHARD
I am dead because of a quota???

RACHAEL
Well, YES. Now MOVE ON!

LAURA
(barging in angrily carrying a clipboard) WHAT IS THE HOLD UP???

RACHAEL
He won't move on? That whole, "Will to live" thing is stopping the whole process!

LAURA
Did you tell him he was to be recycled to a better life???

RACHAEL
YES!

RICHARD
But I don't want to be recycled!

RACHAEL
See?

LAURA
(turning to Richard and smiling very sweetly) Hi Richard.

RICHARD
You're immortal too?

LAURA
(waving him off)
Yes, yes. Now why aren't you moving on?

RICHARD
I am happy with my life! I don't want to move on.

LAURA
(wearing a strained smile then looking at her clipboard) But Richard, you are going to move on to a fantastic life. You are being placed to become a huge Hollywood star! You will be famous! Oh and what and irony! Your last name is Harper and you are to be born in Harper Valley California! Oh and Joy of Joys, you still get to be gay! What more could you ask for?

RICHARD
(clutching the pearls)
Talk about typecasting!

LAURA
(almost as if too herself)
Still, you're no Neil Patrick Harris but you can pull it off.

RICHARD
Wait, no. This is crazy. What about my old life? No. I want my old life back. I was happy in it and Rachael said I was early anyway. They only killed me to fill a quota so you all can have a holiday.

Laura turns and glares at Rachael who shrugs back then turns back to Richard, once again smiling sweetly.

LAURA

Richard, look. We all have our jobs to do here and you are stopping us from fulfilling ours. You have a great life coming and will be very comfortable. So how about we just get you started in that life?

She starts to lead him off and he jerks away.

RICHARD

NO! I don't WANT to die!

LAURA

(now full of rage grabs him by the shirt and jerks him forward close to her face) You listen to me, buster. We haven't had a holiday in over 500 years. 500 YEARS while you little bugs get Christmas and Easter, the fourth of July and Thanksgiving. Don't get me started on the state workers!!! We deserve this holiday and you are going to give it to us or so help me I will make all your lives miserable. You will suffer as no mortal has suffered in the history of your pathetic holiday filled lives. Now, MOVE ON!!

Rachael, standing behind Laura, nods, mimes horns and points, smiling, to Laura.

RICHARD

No! I want to live! I want to live!!

LAURA
(trying to drag him through the door) No you don't!
You just think you do. Now stop making this difficult!

RICHARD
I have friends! I have family!

LAURA
(pushing hard)
They don't love you! NOBODY LOVES YOU!!!

RICHARD
YES they DO!! I am adored by all who know me!

RACHAEL
Ha ha!!

LAURA
(glaring again at Rachael)
HELP ME!

Rachael comes and helps start pushing.

RICHARD
No No NO!!

LAURA
YES YES YES!!

Mark comes into the room.

MARK
What is going on here?

Laura and Rachael straighten up and clear their throats.

LAURA
Nothing?

MARK
What is HE doing here?

LAURA
Well you see, he died and...

MARK
Richard died? He wasn't scheduled to die for another 20 years!

LAURA
Yes but accidents do happen and..

RACHAEL
SHE MADE US DO IT!!! SHE WANTED A HOLIDAY REAL BAD!!! SHE BRIBED US WITH CANDY AND PRETTY CLOTHES!!!

MARK
(looking sternly at Laura)
Is this true?

> LAURA
> (glaring at Rachael again)
> Maybe a little but it's been over 500 years!!

> MARK
> Stop! Stop talking. Richard, go home.

The lights go out and you hear, One Two Three Four Five, Breath. One two three four five, breath then you hear coughing. He's Back!! There is cheering. Lights come up and people are surrounding Richard.

> RICHARD
> Wha...What happened?

> BEANS
> (helping Richard to his feet) You damn near got yourself killed.

> RICHARD
> OMG I was dead! I remember! You were there, (then he points at Rachael) and you were there, (then he sees Laura and points an accusing finger) and YOU!! YOU!!!

Richard runs screaming out of the theater. Everyone follows him trying to catch him. Except Laura.

LAURA
(smiling evilly)
I told you I'd make your life a living hell.

MARK
LAURA!!

LAURA
(looking up to the ceiling and saying in exasperation)
OH. MY GOD. COMING!!!!!!

RETIRING EDWINA

Written by

Laura Vedenhaupt
&
David Walling

Copyright (c) 2012

Cast

JACKIE: A successful business woman in her 40s. She has an information/exercise TV show. Edwina is her mother though her friends have never known.

PENELOPE: Another successful woman in her 40s who is running for Senator.

D.D.: A successful therapist as well as children's book author. Her real name is Dwight David. She's VERY outgoing and not afraid to say anything.

LAURA: A 40 something Jewish mother of two. Happily married to her wonderful husband. Unbeknownst to her friends she's a proctologist. Her maiden name is Assner and her married name is Foote.

EDWINA: A woman in her 60s who is retiring from the college she has been working at for over 20 years. She loves these girls as if they were all her own. She is the mother of Jackie. She's smart, well spoken, and mischievous.

EDDIE: A very young waiter of about 21 to 25. He's a good guy but not very observant. He's great at pouring wine.

INT. COLLEGE HALL - EVENING

Jackie and Penelope enter.

                      JACKIE
            Penelope, look at this! God, I can't believe she's
            finally retiring.

                    PENELOPE
            Let's take our seats.

They go up on stage and take their seats. As they do a waiter comes up to them.

                    EDDIE
            Hi. I'll be your drink server tonight. Would you two
            like some wine?

                    JACKIE
              (holding up her glass)
            That would be wonderful!

                    PENELOPE
              (also holding up her glass)
            Yes please.

Eddie fills them part way up the glass, nods and wanders off.

                    JACKIE
            It's nice that they have our table up on the stage. It's
            easier since we get to speak for her.

PENELOPE
She had a good run. Twenty-some odd years luring undergrads into her class with weird course names.

JACKIE
Remember Persuasive Whining?

PENELOPE
I believe that was the prerequisite for "Jekyl and Seuss: Doctors of Mayhem".

JACKIE
She always tried so hard to make us actually care about literature.

PENELOPE
Wait. I didn't realize you had taken any of her classes.

JACKIE
Actually, there's something I've been wanting to tell you...

D.D. comes in and walks towards their table.

PENELOPE
OH! Before I forget, I wanted to thank you again for auctioning off a spot on your show as a fund-raiser for my re-election campaign. I am going to crush my opponent come election day.

JACKIE
Anything for a friend and everything for a sister.

BOTH
KAPPA DELTA!

D.D.
(swooping in and picking up her glass from the table.)
I'll drink to that! KAPPA DELTA!

JACKIE AND PENELOPE
D.D.!!

Eddie promptly comes over and puts some wine in her glass then leaves.

D.D.
(She waggles her left hand. There is nothing on it.)
Well? What do you think?

JACKIE
What are we looking at?

D.D.
No ring!

PENELOPE
That's a good thing?

                    D.D.
It is when the couple wants different things. I wanted
to rent a house in Malibu for the summer and he
wanted the redhead who owned it.

                    JACKIE
Ouch! How old was she?

                    D.D.
He was 22.

                    LAURA
Who was 22?

                    JACKIE, PENELOPE AND D.D.
LAURA!!

                    LAURA
          (sitting down)
The old place looks great. God it hasn't changed a bit.

As Laura sits down Eddie comes and fills her glass. Jackie downs what is left of hers real quick and tries to get his attention. He doesn't notice and wanders off.

                    JACKIE
          (looking around the girls to see where Eddie is
           going to before looking back at Laura)
I'm having an eighties flashback. You'd think they'd
have remodeled at least once in the last twenty-three
years.

LAURA

Twenty-five for me.

JACKIE

You look great though. In fact, you all do. Okay, fess up. Who's had a little help?

PENELOPE

Help?

JACKIE

Plastic surgery.

PENELOPE

Not me.

LAURA

No way.

D.D.

Boob job. Husband number one paid for them. Of course, that was before he became ex-husband number one.

PENELOPE

Maybe I had a little lipo. Carrying Jennifer was a breeze but Micky demolished my figure.

LAURA
Rhinoplasty. (she gets odd looks from the rest) WHAT? At graduation we get a choice in my family; a car or a nose job. I picked the nose job. Besides, I had a structural defect that affected my breathing.

JACKIE
I remember. We were roomies your senior year. Your snores were legendary. Sounded like.. What did you call it penny?

PENELOPE
I said it sounded like two hogs rasslin' in a waller.

D.D.
What about you, Jacks?

JACKIE
Butt lift.

They all lean back and look at her butt.

PENELOPE
Wow.

D.D.
Nice

LAURA
Very... round.

JACKIE
The rest of me, of course, is all natural.

PENELOPE
Me too.

D.D.
Definitely

LAURA
Completely natural.

JACKIE
...mostly.

PENELOPE
Botox.

D.D.
Laser hair removal.

LAURA
Collagen injections.

JACKIE
Miss Clairol.

PENELOPE
Thank God for Miss Clairol.

LAURA
Love me some Miss Clairol.

D.D.
Coloring our hair is nothing anymore. I'm not even sure what my original color was. The summer before college, I told my Dad I wanted to go blonde with pink accents. He asked, "Why do you want to dye your beautiful hair?" I told him I wanted to stand out, to be an individual, so he let me. When we got to the campus, it was a sea of blonde and pink. Even some of the guys. Dad was a gentleman and didn't say anything about it but he did give me an extra $20 to get my hair re-done. He didn't say what the 20 was for but I knew.

JACKIE
I remember desperately wanting to have my hair feathered. BUT, Mom wasn't having any of it. "Your hair is so beautiful. Why would you want to chop it up into different lengths? You can't do anything with it - can't wear it in a ponytail or French braid or a bun. All the choppy ends will stick out and you'll look like you have feathers IN your hair!"

LAURA
I always wanted bangs. I'd had straight hair parted down the middle for years, so freshmen year of college, I got bangs, ratted them, then used about half a bottle of Aqua-Net to get them to stand up. A few years later, "There's Something About Mary" came

out in theaters. I never ratted my bangs again.

PENELOPE
Mama was always after me to wear my hair in a bun. She said it looked grown up. A bun? Seriously! What teenager wants to wear a bun, especially just starting college? I wanted to look grown up, sure, but not geriatric. Great-Grandma Bennett had hair that swept the length of the floor. She wore it in a bun on top of her head. I thought it looked like a cow pie. Do you all remember the mole craze?

JACKIE
Moles?

LAURA
What are you talking about?

PENELOPE
Y'all know I've always had these moles on my face.

JACKIE, LAURA, D.D.

Yeah. Sure. Uh huh...

PENELOPE

Mama always called them beauty marks so I had never been self-conscious about them. Somewhere about my Junior year, and quite suddenly, those stick-on moles became the "in" thing. Girls could put them anywhere. Mine, of course, wouldn't move. More than one fashionista felt the need to point out that (done in a snooty voice) the entire purpose of stick-on moles was to be able to change your look instantly. (end voice). So I started putting different shades of eye shadow on my beauty marks. You know, just to change things up. Mama took me to the doctor because she was sure I had melanoma.

JACKIE
Your poor mother!

LAURA
We were so vain back then.

D.D.
Not me. I was just being realistic.

JACKIE, LAURA, PENELOPE
(Jackie, while she is speaking is trying to get Eddie's attention to no avail)
Yeah, right. Sure you were.

LAURA
You know, speaking of makeup, I always used to think my eyes were too small. There was a girl in my ethics class who had eyes like a goldfish. You know the ones. The ones that have the eyes bulge out the sides of their heads? Anyway, I decided to enhance my eyes with makeup, and what attracts the eye more than glitter? I'll tell you what attracts the eye more than glitter. Eyes that are allergic to glitter makeup, that's what. You think those goldfish eyes are gross? Imagine seeing them on a person. My eyelids looked like puffy red marshmallows.

D.D.
Nasty!

JACKIE
Oh...gross.

LAURA
I KNOW! The doctor thought I'd been punched in the face and that I just didn't want to tell my parents. Oy, to be so lucky as to get punched. At least then I wouldn't have had to listen to my mother lecture me on appropriate makeup for my (hand quotes) "delicate skin".

PENELOPE
Can you blame her? What would you tell YOUR daughter?

LAURA
That I'm a cool mother and she can walk around with goldfish eyes all she wants.

All of them laugh

D.D.
Talking about fashion, you all aren't going to believe what kind of fashion quirk I was into.

JACKIE
I wouldn't bank on that.

PENELOPE
Neither would I.

Laura laughs.

D.D.
(grinning)
You are TERRIBLE friends. Just terrible. Now let me tell you. When I was sixteen I wanted stonewashed jeans. Guess or Jordache, I wasn't picky. Dad and I searched the yard sales for a used pair. We couldn't find any so we went to the store where dad bought me a pair of no-name jeans. I cried all the way home because not only were they no-names but they weren't even stonewashed. Dad never had much money so he figured he could MAKE stonewashed jeans all by himself. That man took those new blue jeans and spent an entire weekend washing them over and over

again. He left out the stone part and they never really faded. Finally late Sunday night he brought out the bleach.

ALL
(gasping)
No! The horror! He didn't!

D.D.
Yes he did! I couldn't stand the thought of wearing those splotchy things out in public but he had worked so hard on them. It was his proud smile as he held them out to me that made me put them on. I figured it was just one day, how bad could it be?

PENELOPE
Was it pretty bad?

D.D.
Not at all. I never received more compliments on an outfit in my life. Everyone was asking where they could buy those amazing jeans. I said I didn't know. They were a gift from my father.

LAURA
See? Se how things work out for the better?

JACKIE
That was really nice.

D.D.

Yeah. It was wonderful. What about you, Jackie? You have a fashion disaster story for us?

JACKIE

Oh I am sure I can think up one. Lemme see. Oh yeah! I know you'll find this hard to believe but when I was in high school, I was a horrible nail-biter. But it's the eighties and Lee Press-on nails had finally arrived. It didn't matter anymore if you routinely gnawed off your nails. Those wonderful little bits of plastic covered a multitude of sins. My mother HATED them. I think she preferred me chewing my nails off to wearing fake ones. Naturally, I chose that time as my fashion rebellion period. It was the night of my senior prom. I'm in this gorgeous metallic blue dress which was beautifully accented by my press-on glamour length nails. Mom said I looked like a dolled-up Freddy Krueger.

D.D.

HA! That's hilarious.

PENELOPE

I could see that.

JACKIE
Danny and I were headed inside when the wind picked up. My mom didn't believe in Aqua-net at that age either. I grabbed my dress with one hand and my hair with the other. I lost my balance and down I went. Poor Danny was trying to help me up when I found that my nails had gotten tangled in my hair somehow. I yanked hard and huge strands came out with them. I lost my balance again and we both went down. Somehow, in all the ruckus, I scratched Danny's face. We finally got up. My hair was a wreck, my dress was wrinkled, Danny was bleeding, and the principle wouldn't let us into the prom.

PENELOPE
Oh no!

LAURA
Because you were a little bit frumpled?

JACKIE
Yeah. He said it looked like we had too much fun already!

D.D.
So, you missed your prom?

JACKIE
No. It took a bit of arguing and a lot of convincing, but he finally let us in.

LAURA
Well that's good.

D.D.
You still had a good time then.

JACKIE
Oh yeah. We danced with catlike grace across the dance floor.

D.D.
Nice!

LAURA
A nice happy ending.

PENELOPE
Good for you! (she looks thoughtful for a moment) Hey, do you all remember Jack?

JACKIE
(wrinkling her nose)
He was scrawny.

LAURA
(holding hers)
He was stinky.

D.D.
He couldn't walk straight.

PENELOPE
He's dead.

Everyone gasps and gives their condolences.

D.D.
What happened?

PENELOPE
Remember when he had to have is teeth pulled because they were rotten?

JACKIE
12 of them, right?

LAURA
At least he didn't stink anymore.

PENELOPE
Afterward, when he'd lay on top of me, he'd drool.

ALL
EWWWWWW!

JACKIE
Remember what he did with his tongue?

LAURA
It was disgusting.

                    D.D.
It was funny.

                    PENELOPE
          (pulling out a picture and shows everyone)
I have a picture!

                    JACKIE
          (sniffling a bit)
I loved that cat.

                    D.D.
Pulls a Kleenex out of her bra and dabs her eyes.

                    LAURA
I hated that cat.

                    PENELOPE
I miss that cat.

                    D.D.
Let's drink to that cat.

They all toast to the cat except for Jackie who toasts with a dry glass then desperately trying to find Eddie.

                    D.D. (cont'd)
So, Jackie, what's been going on with you all these years?

JACKIE

You all know I lost Danny in Iraq. I had been working as the P.E. Teacher at the local grade school. After Danny died I needed a change and, well, ended up with my own TV show. "Get Less with Moore". It's part talk show, part exercise program.

LAURA

Using the spelling of your last name as the more in Less is Moore, I presume? Clever.

PENELOPE

I am glad you didn't give in and you pushed yourself along. That spot on your show will go a long way in my Senate run.

JACKIE

Ah. You know me. I'm always happy to help. You just keep writing checks to the Jeff City Day Care Center and you can have all the air time you need.

LAURA

Jefferson City Day Care? What's that?

JACKIE

It's a non-profit United Way Agency. They help families with the ridiculously high cost of day care. It's really difficult for many families today to work and find a fun and safe place for their kids that they can actually afford, especially single moms and dads. I don't know how they do it.

PENELOPE
They also have an amazing Early Childhood program.

JACKIE
I really love what they are trying to do so I do what I can to help.

LAURA
Sounds impressive! Give me the address before we leave today so I can donate.

PENELOPE
She let me have airtime on her show for my campaign in exchange for taking the time to learn about it which is how I got involved.

D.D.
(reaching into her bra)
Here's 20 bucks.

JACKIE
Good lord. How much stuff do you have in there?

D.D.
You'll never guess.

JACKIE
Toothbrush?

LAURA
Toothpaste?

PENELOPE
Lipstick!

JACKIE
MORE KLEENEX!!

LAURA
Credit Cards

PENELOPE
Tampons!

JACKIE
Driver's License!

LAURA
Tic-Tacs!

PENELOPE
Mace!

D.D.
You all are a bunch of freaks! (She pauses looking down her shirt) The only thing you missed was the hand sanitizer.

LAURA
(kinda peeking)
You actually have a toothbrush down there?

D.D.
Of course! I have to keep my pearly whites pearly white.

JACKIE
Why don't you just carry a purse like a normal human being?

D.D.
The strap hurts my arm.

JACKIE
Only you. Okay, D.D., let's hear it. What have YOU been up to the last 20 years.

D.D.
Oh please. My life is boring.

ALL AT THE SAME TIME
JACKIE: HA! LAURA: LIAR PENELOPE: NO WAY!

D.D.
Okay. I've been married four times.

PENELOPE
Wow.

JACKIE
I thought you were a therapist.

                    D.D.
I didn't say I was a marriage counselor, did I? No.
Right after graduate school I married a guy by the
name of John Stilts. He turned out to be a chauvinist
pig who wanted a mother, not a wife. He did give me
these though.

D.D. Sticks out her chest.

                    LAURA
Very generous.

                    D.D.
I know! We divorced three years later. After John
there was Paul. Paul Strickland. He owned a vineyard.
He was such a lovely man.

                    JACKIE
Sooo, how long before you divorced HIM?

                    D.D.
Oh, I didn't divorce him. I killed him.

Everyone sits stunned for a second.

                    JACKIE
WHAT? Oh, my God. What the hell happened?

D.D.
We owned a small vineyard at the time and he kept his work boots in the hall closet. One days he worked in the fields, he always dropped his boots off there before he came the rest of the way into the house. One day I hid in the closet wearing nothing but a big red bow. When he opened the door. I jumped out and yelled, "Take me now!"

PENELOPE
Oh. Heart attack?

LAURA
Stroke?

D.D.
No, no. Nothing like that. Unbeknownst to me he had popped a bunch of grapes from the new field into his mouth. When I jumped out at him he breathed in and...there ya have it.

LAURA
That's tragic.

PENELOPE
That's terrible.

JACKIE
That sounds just like you.

D.D.
(stares at Jackie for a moment)
ANYWAY, it was a few years later that I met and married George...something.

LAURA
Something?

PENELOPE
You don't' remember your husband's name?

D.D.
Honey, it was a Vegas wedding and what happens in Vegas stays in Vegas.

JACKIE
Did you kill him too?

D.D.
No! Of course not. We had it annulled when the Bacardi dried up. So then there was...

PENELOPE
Ringo?

Everyone looks questioningly at her.

PENELOPE (cont'd)
You know! John, Paul. George? HELLO? The Beatles? Oh, come on!! That's funny.

D.D.
NO! GEEZ!!! Do you remember Harry Drinsel?

PENELOPE
Scary Harry?

JACKIE
With the nasty eyebrows?

ALL EXCEPT D.D.
EWWWWWWW!!!

D.D.
(feigning exasperation)
Do you want to hear this or not?

LAURA
We're all ears.

D.D.
If you were I'd have finished my story by now. So, I married Harry...

ALL EXCEPT D.D.
EWWWWW!!!

D.D.
Are we twelve? Seriously? We got married. We got divorced. The papers were signed last week and I am a free woman. We really should have called him Fairy Harry.

LAURA
Why?

D.D.
He wasn't scary at all. Especially in a tutu and leotards.

ALL EXCEPT D.D.
Oh, my. Holy crap. Wow.

D.D.
(waving them off)
Penny, what about you and Walter?

PENELOPE
Walter and I celebrated our 15th anniversary last month. The kids stayed with Aunt Jackie and Walt and I went to the beach for the weekend. It was so romantic.

LAURA
Did you have your, "from Here to Eternity" moment?

PENELOPE
Well if you mean did we make love on the sand? No. If you mean did we walk hand in hand down the beach with the waves caressing our ankles until Walter cuts his foot on a broken seashell, I trip over a bunch of seaweed and he takes off running toward the house screaming, "SHARK! SHARK!" then yes. It sure felt like an eternity.

LAURA
That's awful.

PENELOPE
What's awful is that hit was a public beach. That crazy man damn near started a stampede of half-naked people! It was not pretty. Now you've heard MY life's story, let's hear Laura's.

D.D.
First, I need a refill.

JACKIE
Speaking of, who the hell do you have to sleep with around here to get a drink?

D.D.
Well there's Mark, or Brian. Oh, and there's always Eddie.

D.D. Waves down Eddie and he comes and fills everyone's glass but Jackie's right before she says...

JACKIE
Isn't Eddie a little young even for you?

Eddie looks panic stricken and hurries off. Jackie gapes holding her empty glass in the air.

D.D.
(grinning)
Okay, maybe not Eddie.

PENELOPE
Let's get back to the subject at hand ladies.   Laura?

LAURA
What?

JACKIE
Go on. Out with it.

LAURA
Fine. There's not much to tell. I graduated, I studied medicine, did my internship, got married, had babies and here I am.

JACKIE
That's it? REALLY?

LAURA
What more is there to tell?

PENELOPE
Well, who you married for one thing.

LAURA
Melvin. Oh, he was a dream boat. His wavy hair, his scrawny lightly muscled body. Just a doll.

D.D.
Lightly muscled?

LAURA
That's what I said. Who needs all those lumps? Anyway, he converted to Judaism, we got married and we had two beautiful children. All of you would know all this if you if you knew how to write a letter.

JACKIE
Tell us about your kids.

LAURA
Oy Vey. Jacob was the first born. The apple of his father's eye he is. Looks just like 'em. Ruth was second. She has her grandmother's temper and her father's hair.

PENELOPE
They sound absolutely lovely.

LAURA
You'd think so, wouldn't you? You'd think they would know how to call their mother. The woman who fed them day in and day out for 18 years. I washed their clothes and cleaned and cooked and do I get so much as a card? No. I have to call and beg for one. Now is that right, I ask you? Jacob, the other day, comes to me and he says to stop bugging him that he doesn't want to date a Jewish girl. I says, "Why not? Are you ashamed of being Jewish", I says. He tells me no, but

he thinks Jewish women are the living embodiment of guilt.

      D.D.
HA!

Penelope claps her hand over her mouth to keep from laughing outloud.

      JACKIE
Oh, my.

      LAURA
I know! I says to him, "Jacob", I says, "You're breaking my heart. I held you in my womb for nine months. I suffered through the birthing of you even with that giant head because I love you so much and still you break my heart." I don't know why he says such things.

      JACKIE, PENELOPE AND D.D.
I can't imagine. Kids! No clue.

      JACKIE
What do they do now? Are they in college?

      LAURA
Jacob, he's a buyer.

      D.D.
He's bi?

LAURA
ER! Buy-ER. You know, for one of those big chain stores. Ruth she's going to school to be a podiatrist.

PENELOPE
Very nice.

D.D.
I'll drink to that!

D.D. Drinks her drink really quick and waves the waiter over. Jackie, once again, tries to get his attention for a refill and fails.

PENELOPE
You must be proud!

LAURA
Oh I am. Melvin's proud too. He likes to joke that because of him they aren't full-blooded Jews. They are Jew-ISH.

Mark, the announcer comes out to the stage and clears his throat for audience attention.

MARK
Ladies and gentlemen. (INSERT EXTRA DIALOGUE HERE SUCH AS ABOUT YOUR PLAYHOUSE) It is now my pleasure to introduce to you our guest of honor, Dr. Edwina Emerson.

Claps and hugs all around as she comes out.

EDWINA

Thank you everyone for that wonderful reception. A special thank you to Mark for your efforts. Mark is a man who does not know the meaning of an impossible task, who does not know the meaning of taking a break and who does not understand the meaning of the word no. So we all pitched in and bought him a dictionary.

Edwina waits for laughter to die down a bit before continuing.

EDWINA (cont'd)

I am honored to see so many friends and family here tonight. To the ladies to the right (or left) of me you have shared the joys and heartbreaks of your lives with me and for that I thank you. When I was preparing my speech for this evening, I tried to take the advice of Friedrich Nietzsche. "To say in ten sentences what others say in a whole book." DAMN, I just wasted two sentences. There goes another one! Forget this.

Edwina tosses her speech aside.

PENELOPE

I can't believe you are using that old joke again. I remember that from every class I ever took from you.

EDWINA

Shall I tell everyone what I remember about YOU, Miss PMS? I remember you in front of the debate team. You were dressed in a black onesie, a hot pink muscle shirt and plaid leg-warmers using that "Old Joke" as an icebreaker.

JACKIE

I think the shirt was the icebreaker. Who could be intimidated by that?

EDWINA

It took a strong woman to argue the pro side of a dress code requiring student uniforms. Especially wearing that, and I use the term loosely, outfit.

PENELOPE

I got that from you, you know. Not the outfit! Strength. That debate was scheduled the same week as my mother's heart surgery. I'd never lost a debate before and now I was going to have to forfeit. I didn't know how you understood what I was saying with all the crying and nose-blowing going on but you did. You talked to me about choice and responsibility; about family.

EDWINA

About the fact that Kappa Delta's Great Hall had enough room for both debate teams and judges.

PENELOPE

Yes. I checked the debate by-laws then marched over to the academic affairs office. I convinced them to reschedule the debate. The point is, preparation and perseverance won me that debate and I got to be with my family when they needed me. It didn't matter what I was wearing.

D.D.

Thank God.

PENELOPE

(throwing D.D. a knowing look then turning back to Edwina and pulling out a dagger charm)

The Spirit of Kappa Delta sorority is symbolized, in part, by a dagger. In ancient times this was used to markup manuscripts - kind of like the way you used to mark up our term papers, except y'all used red ink. More recently, the dagger represents a leader or guardian. I can't think of anything more appropriate to express what you mean to me. Thank you.

EDWINA

I've always thought of you as a daughter. All of you as my daughters.

D.D.
(Standing up)
And we've always thought of you as SOME kind of mother. I remember coming to class hung over and other times skipping altogether. I never figured out how you knew when I'd had a little too much to drink and when I was actually sick or just faking. (Jackie looks a bit uncomfortable.) I guess mothers have that knack.

EDWINA
I was worried about you. I didn't want you to waste your life drinking.

D.D.
Trust me, (she takes a drink and smiles) it is not wasted.

EDWINA
Do you remember what I would do every time you came to class hung over?

D.D.
Torture me with stories about greasy food and blood sausage.

EDWINA
I torture because I care.

D.D.

You were the mother I never had. You pushed me to be better than I thought I ever could be. (to the audience) Because of this woman, I survived some horrific losses. My father, my home, and, for a little while, my marbles. (turns back to Edwina). You talked with me when I couldn't talk to anyone, not even my sisters. You helped me find my voice. You helped me find a great Beaujolais... Well, Anyway. Without you I wouldn't have what I have today. (Looks around and at the ceiling). A vineyard with a winery that looks very much like this school. (She looks back at Edwina) The spirit of the Kappa Delta Sorority is symbolized, in part, by a Katydid. While disgusting, the little guy represents life, death, and rebirth. I can't think of anything more appropriate to express what you mean to me. Thank you. (Presents her with a second charm).

EDWINA

(giving her a hug)

Thank you, my dear. (Turns to the audience) For those of you who don't know, not only is D.D,. A respected therapist, she is also a best-selling author of children's books.

JACKIE

But don't look for the name D.D. Look for Dwight David.

D.D.
(looking surprised and horrified)
How did you know that?

PENELOPE
Is that your pen name?

D.D.
(snaps her fingers and the waiter comes over quickly to give her a refill. Jackie tries but does not get his attention. D.D. clears her throat)
My grandfather served under Eisenhower in World War II. He told stories about what a great man the General was. My father promised Grandpa that he would name his firstborn after Ike.

LAURA
Aren't you the first born?

D.D.
Yes, yes! My name is Dwight David Bishop, Okay? I didn't tell you guys because I didn't want you to make fun of me then.

JACKIE
(laughing)
You think we're not going to make fun of you now?

EDWINA
Ahem. If I may continue? Dr. Bishop's books help children to understand and work through Issues that could break most of us. I brought a copy of each of these with me tonight and I would be honored if you would autograph them for me before you leave.

LAURA
(half whispering to the girls)
Look and see if she has a pen in there.

D.D. pulls out a pen from her bra and clicks it, ready to go.

LAURA (cont'd)
Oh my God. That must be why they call it a wonder bra.

EDWINA
Laura, I have to ask. What's with the name card? Why not Dr. Laura Assner?

LAURA
Well my married name is Foote.

JACKIE
So, you went from an ass to a foot?

                    LAURA
NER! ASS-NER!! How many times do I have to tell you people? As I was saying earlier, I married Mel and after I graduated medical school, people started calling thinking I was a podiatrist. So, I put Dr. Laura on my business cards and advertisements. Now people call me for psychological advice.

D.D. Snorts into her wine glass while Jackie tries to get the waiter's attention again.

                    LAURA (cont'd)
Professor, you know this, but I don't think anyone else does. When I started school, I was going to be an accountant.

                    D.D.
But you suck at math.

                    LAURA
Shut up Dwight! What you say is true. Drunken, but true. I was terrible at math. Not only did Professor Ed tutor me but she also knew how unhappy I was. I didn't want to be an accountant. That was what my parents wanted. (to Edwina). You helped me realize that I could never make anyone else happy if I wasn't happy with myself, so I ditched accounting and enrolled in pre-med. No more staring at numbers all day. Now I take care of assholes.

PENELOPE
You're a bouncer?

LAURA
Lord no! I'm a proctologist.

D.D.
I should have called you about Johnny.

PENELOPE
Proctologist?!?

They all start laughing.

LAURA
What's so funny?

ALL EXCEPT LAURA
ASSNER!!

The laughter trickles away as Laura presents Edwina with her charm for the bracelet.

LAURA
The spirit of Kappa Delta sorority is symbolized, in part, by the Nautilus. The shell, not the ship. The Nautilus represents renewal and expanding beyond your horizons. I can't think of anything more appropriate to express what you mean to me. Thank you.

EDWINA
(hugging Laura)
Oh my dear, thank YOU! You and the other girls have given me such great joy and great pride. There were days when I felt as if I couldn't teach one more young slacker, then you girls game along. You not only filled my heart, but you gave me hope for the future and the reassurance that I was doing the right thing. A professor doesn't always know how well they have done or what influence they have on the people they teach. I am glad to have had each of you in my classes and later as friends. You all have been and are a great strength not only unto yourselves but to those who know you.

Edwina pauses and looks to the audience.

EDWINA (cont'd)
I would like to thank...

JACKIE
(Standing up quickly)
WAIT! Wait. I have something to say.

EDWINA
The floor is yours, my dear.

JACKIE
The spirit of the Kappa Delta sorority is symbolized in part by the teddy bear, which represents gentleness, security, and nanny cams. I can't think of anything

more appropriate to express what you mean to me. (She turns towards the other girls.) You girls know that my mother was an inspiration for a popular sitcom. The main character was based, in part, on my mother's early years as a designer. You also know she was a consultant on the show for years. What I didn't tell you was, that due to divorce, we had different last names which is why you could never find her in the credits. Well, that and she went under a pseudonym at the time. There's a reason, in all the time we've been friends, you've never met my mother. When I was in college, I asked my mother to grant me a wish. I asked her to treat me as if I were a stranger. It was a foolish request, and I'm sure it caused her much pain. During times that should have been filled with a mother's pride and love, she was reduced to cool silence. It's about time I publicly apologize to her for my hurtful wish and to my friends for keeping this from them.

Jackie turns to Edwina and takes a deep breath as the girls look at each other in surprise.

                JACKIE (cont'd)

I'm sorry, Mom. I know you understood that I wanted the other students to like me for me and not for who my mother was. I underestimated my friends and I underestimated how very much I wish you could have been beside me all those times the other parents were there.

PENELOPE
Holy Sh-cow!

D.D.
What? SHE'S YOUR MOM? (she downs her drink)

Eddie comes by and refills it while Jackie tries to get his attention and when he walks away gives him a dirty look.

LAURA
You couldn't even tell US? We're like family! Except for the not being Jewish part!

JACKIE
I know. I apologize to all of you. Mostly to you, Mom.

EDWINA
    (hurrying to Jackie and hugging her. She then
    holds her at arm's length with a smile)
Oh darling. I didn't miss anything. I was always there. At the sorority functions, at your graduation. I was the faculty adviser, so it was expected, but still, I would not have missed any of that for the world. I carry your heart with me, I carry it in my heart. I am never without it. Anywhere I go you go, my dear; and whatever is done by only me is your doing, my darling.

PENELOPE
WOOO! It's E.E. Cummings!

JACKIE
Here is the deepest secret nobody knows. Here is the root of the root and the bud of the bud and the sky of the sky of a tree called life; which grows higher than soul can hope, or mind can hide and this is the wonder that's keeping the stars apart.

JACKIE AND EDWINA TOGETHER
I carry your heart, I carry it in my heart.

They embrace again and after a few moments separate and wipe their eyes. Jackie goes and sits down while Edwina goes back to the podium.

EDWINA
You all have been like daughters all these years. I thank you for joining my class, for being inspiring, for sharing the struggles and the laughter of your lives. You kept an aging professor young for many years.

She turns back towards the audience

EDWINA (cont'd)
I would like to thank all of you for coming. I have been proud to serve this university for 27 years. I would be proud to serve another 27, were it not that the young need the spot I hold. I have other endeavors that I will now have time to pursue. Like spending more time with my daughter and her militant exercise regimen. I can feel the exhaustion

seeping in already.

JACKIE
HEY! That exhausting exercise regimen is keeping you alive, Old Woman!

EDWINA
(laughing)
Indeed, it is. I would like to thank you again for being here. Thank you for honoring me in the twilight of my academic life. I have been blessed. I would like to share with you a poem that I believe reflects the teaching profession and the correlation it has between the teacher and the ones being taught. The author is unknown and the title is "A Teacher's Prayer"

Edwina pauses and clears her throat (perhaps takes a drink if there is water at the podium)

EDWINA (cont'd)
Lord, please help me to strengthen their voices, bodies and minds... To express their feeling and control them sometimes... to explore what's near and venture afar... but most important, to love who they are.

Edwina pauses again, looks at the girls and smiles.

EDWINA (cont'd)
It is not always easy to teach or be taught. Many obstacles stand in the way that need to be overcome.

>   Be gentle with each other. Be patient and most of all
>   be compassionate and giving. Just a little bit of
>   giving goes a long way in anyone's life. Thank you.

Eddie, at this point, is starting to walk by with another bottle of wine.

>   D.D.
>   We can all drink to that!

Jackie jumps up, grabs Eddie by the arm and spins him around. She bends him backwards over the table and grabs the bottle, holds it up triumphantly as the girls hold up their glasses and takes a swig as they all drink.

>   ALL
>   CHEERS!!!